School Rule

School Rule

A Case Study of Participation in
Budgeting in America

Miriam E. David
University of Bristol

formerly at
Harvard Graduate School of Education

Ballinger Publishing Company ● **Cambridge, Mass.**
A Subsidiary of J.B. Lippincott Company

International Standard Book Number: 0-88410-160-6

Library of Congress Catalog Card Number: 74-23863

Printed in the United States of America

Library of Congress Cataloging in Publication Data

David, Miriam E
  School rule.

  Includes bibliographical references.
  1. School districts—United States—Finance. 2. Schools—Accounting.
I. Title.
LB2830.D3   379'.123'0973   74-23863
ISBN 0-88410-160-6

Dedication

To my mother who, much against her wishes, gave me my interest in education, and to my father who, by his example, imbued me with a strong work ethic.

Contents

List of Tables

Foreword

We are at the end of one cycle of reform in the United States, and perhaps not far from the beginning of a new one. In the last cycle, which ran from 1961 to 1971, education was given a prominent role indeed. It was expected to contribute to the overcoming of poverty and inequality, and it itself was to undergo transformation in order to contribute to these major goals. We are now somewhat doubtful as to how much education can, under the best circumstances, contribute to the overcoming of social problems, and equally doubtful as to whether a transformed or reformed educational system is necessary or possible. As Miriam David points out, education was to be transformed by means of citizen participation, decentralization, and local control: this was to make it a more effective instrument for the transmission of basic skills and talents, so that individuals could raise themselves from poverty and the inequalities in cities could somewhat be evened out. Further, the increased level of citizen participation was seen as a good in itself.

Ironically, American school systems—except for those in the large cities—have always been models of local control, citizen participation, and decentralization. But with what effects? Ms. David, who had studied local planning for education in England, came here to conduct a parallel study of American local education authorities. She concentrated on the question of how citizen participation affects the making of the school budget. The selection of topic is not unimportant. The budget is the crucial controlling instrument of modern bureaucratic organizations. It records the changing pattern of power, commitment, and hope. The four communities she chose to study differed in size (but all were small—smaller indeed than any one of the school districts of the now decentralized New York City system), in social and economic characteristics, and in form of government. Two, indeed, retain that anomaly in democratic government, direct democracy by all the citizens of a town. If citizen control means anything at all, it should mean something in these towns, at least the smaller of them, and it should mean something in that area of key interest, the schools.

Does it mean something? Not very much, apparently. Most of the money in the school budget goes for teachers, and is now settled increasingly through collective bargaining. Thus the greater part of the budget is outside the hands of the citizens—unless presumably they rebel against the contract and refuse to fulfill it. This may occur, but there are as yet no examples. The budget also reflects the educational program, but on the whole the citizenry is quiescent. And the elected school committees seem to be quiescent, too, accepting the leadership of the superintendent. The fact is, we are told, we live in a specialized and bureaucratic society, and one expert does not interfere much in another expert's realm.

Does it then mean nothing? Ms. David does not say that either. The citizenry *could* act if it were so inclined. The elected school committee could act more forcefully, too, if it were so inclined. And there are differences among her towns in the degree to which school superintendent leadership is accepted. This is not to conclude that the citizens of each of the towns she has studied are satisfied with what goes on in their schools, but it is to conclude that they are not so dissatisfied that they are willing to resort to organizing and using the latent power the system gives them.

Democracy in a modern bureaucratic state with a professionalized work force, Ms. David is telling us, is no simple thing, and we cannot expect the full-time or even very much of the part-time involvement of the citizenry, even when they formally possess the power of intervention, and even in areas as significant to them as the schools. But this does not mean that democracy is a fraud: it means we must become soberly aware of the limitations on citizen participation in an exceedingly complex society, where various levels of government, bodies of professionals, and bureaucratic organizations, all protected by law and custom, participate in the process of government. "In present complex societies it cannot be expected that citizens would do more than adjudicate on the efficacy and efficiency of a school system," Ms. David concludes. Perhaps we should be grateful for this much.

Nathan Glazer

Acknowledgments

This book is a result of a research study, carried out duirng the year that I spent as visiting research associate at the Harvard Graduate School of Education. It was financed by the Social Science Research Council in England and sponsored by Professor Maurice Peston of the Department of Economics at Queen Mary College, London University. The study arose out of several concerns. In particular, it was the direct outcome of a three-year research study, centered at Queen Mary College and financed by the Department of Education and Science, into educational planning in local authorities in England. The prospects for educational change in England appeared slight because of the complexity and profusion of government machinery at the central and local levels. The question was raised as to whether other countries fared better in responding to citizens' needs. What kinds of machinery, especially to finance education, would work more responsively and equitably?

The focus of my research changed somewhat as a result of my first encounters at Harvard. Nathan Glazer, David Cohen, and Mary Jo Bane pointed the way to a study that would link more usefully with current American interests. They themselves were, at that time, deeply concerned about the problems of bureaucracy in education. Henry Acland, a fellow Britisher at Harvard, helped to marry the British and American concerns. Gerry Murphy and Herold Hunt convinced me of the problems of trying to look at the web of federal, state, and local machinery and guided me to a more local study. To all my colleagues at Harvard I am deeply grateful for the help they gave me in the initial stages of research design. For support and help throughout the stages of data collection and analysis, and for reading and commenting on drafts of the study, I would also like to thank Henry Acland, Mary Jo Bane, Geoff Bock, Sam Bowles, David Cohen, Herb Gintis, Christopher Jencks, Gerry Murphy, Heather Weiss and, in England, Maurice Peston, Brian Neve, Phoebe Hall, Hilary

Land, Roy Parker and my husband, Robert Reiner. Nathan Glazer has proved a constant and particularly kind mentor. For typing the various manuscripts thanks to Kathleen Brookes, Mollie Lucas, and Trixie Hewlett.

      The study could not have been achieved without the cooperation of many people in the four school districts. The four superintendents gave generously of their valuable time, and I should like to thank most warmly Drs. Creedon, Goodman, Quin, and Wood. They certainly more than helped to make my stay in America a rich and fascinating experience. They also put me in touch with their colleagues who, in turn, gave unselfishly of their time. The school committee members gave me most fascinating and uniquely American hospitality by allowing me to observe them in action and to interview them. Thanks to them all. Two newspaper reporters, Barbara Mergurian and Paul Mindus, also provided me with valuable insights into the workings of American education in their communities and gladly commented on drafts of my work. Last, but certainly not least, my three roommates for the year—who had been or were teaching school—Bruce Brand, Barry and Judy Growe, gave the emotional support to continue with what at times seemed like a most impossible task: to understand an unostensibly but increasingly foreign and curious society. For all the mistakes and misunderstandings I accept full responsibility.

Chapter One

Participation and Professionalism: The Problem in Education

Debate about social welfare reforms in America in the sixties centered upon two issues. One was what specific programs should be provided to alleviate the problems of the poor, and of racial and ethnic minorities. The other was how the programs should be administered. "Maximum feasible participation" would be the method of delivering social services.[1] Therefore, social action programs which would involve community groups in decisions about their social welfare were devised. One result was that participation became not only a means of effecting reform but also an end in itself. Racial and ethnic minorities began to advocate wide-scale community control to alleviate all their social problems.[2] However, by the end of the decade, reformers were considerably disillusioned with their notion of participation, partly because it was deemed ineffective and partly because it came to be seen as a paternalistic imposition from above and did not in itself facilitate community involvement.[3]

A major component of the argument for community control by racial and ethnic minorities, which developed out of the federal programs, was the assumption that the more fortunate strata of society already enjoyed such control over their lives.[4] It is the purpose of this study to argue that such control is a myth and that effective involvement of citizens in decision-making requires far more than narrowly conceived organizational changes. To examine the issue it was decided to concentrate on an institutional area which constitutes a critical case. This is to say that an area was chosen where the likelihood of effective citizen participation being realized would be the greatest. The American education system was therefore selected, for it was originally designed to allow for citizen rather than professional control. Indeed, the advocates of community control also made their first demands for changes in their educational system precisely because of this.[5] The disparities between the situation of racial and ethnic minorities and middle-class, white suburbs were ostensibly very great.

THE ORGANIZATION OF
AMERICAN EDUCATION

Education in America was originally conceived as a necessary investment for social and economic development. It was the means to achieve social integration and to service the labor force. But education was not organized at the federal level. Rather, each residential community would choose its own form of education.

In the late nineteenth century, school boards were created as special bodies with autonomous functions.[6] Powers over education were removed from local municipal officials on the premise that education was above politics and should not be subject to the vagaries of partisan political choice. But school boards were to be democratically chosen bodies. Representatives would usually be elected on a non-partisan basis to serve the educational interests of each community. The number of elected representatives on each board was small, about five to ten members. The reason for the reform was to ensure both an effective and efficient education system, divorced from political intrigue.[7]

The system has not changed radically since this major reform.[8] School boards or committees still serve individual districts and are responsible for elementary and secondary education: the curricula and programs, hiring and firing of staff and their salaries, and the operation and maintenance of buildings. Traditionally, the states have only played a marginal role in educational policy-making, although education was conceived as a state function.[9] The states have provided some financial support and established minimum standards of provision such as buildings and teacher certification, the extent of which varies between states. On the whole, legislatures have delegated major responsibility to the constituent school districts.

The federal government also has not exerted any control over educational policies. One of its first major interventions was the seminal Elementary and Secondary Education Act of 1965.[10] But even this act related to only marginal rather than core programs. Basically it provided financial aid to poor districts or categories of children and for educational innovations. Since then the government has provided aid for school lunch programs.

Most finance for education is obtained locally, through a tax on property. Since communities vary in the value of their properties, the money available for education in each community is not the same. It also varies according to the willingness of each community to tax itself. The state often makes an effort to reduce disparities between communities with equalization formulae and often by allocating additional revenue. State contributions have usually been less than half of that expended by any school district. There is, however, no mechanism for reducing interstate variation.[11] The legal system, which has always been used to determine aspects of educational problems, has also been involved in this problem. In the last half decade, state and federal courts have been used in an attempt to reduce inequities in resources and spending, through the now famous Serrano and Rodriguez cases.[12] Although several state courts declared the use of property taxes to finance education inequitable, the federal court over the Rodriguez case did not find the system to be in violation of the U.S. Constitution.

The existing organization, although there is no single prevailing government machinery for all states, appears to lend itself to citizen control of decisions either by elected representatives or participants from the community. As a result of demographic trends in the last two decades of "the retreat from the inner cities" and suburban migration, the predominant pattern is one of small school districts of about 30,000 in population. In 1966 there were 31,706 separate educational authorities.[13]

The form of organization is endorsed by legal decisions and proposals for reform. Moves to create a larger metropolitan area by amalgamation in Richmond, Virginia and Detroit, Michigan, to aid school desegregation were defeated in the federal courts. A proposal to increase citizen choice of education has been to provide parents with educational vouchers for them each to decide which school their children would attend.[14] Although the organization of the system is apparently designed to provide machinery for citizen participation and control, it is the argument of this book that effective control is in the hands of the professional educators.

PROFESSIONAL CONTROL IN EDUCATION

This situation reflects an organizational principle in direct competition to that of participatory democracy, which has been influential in determining the development of the educational system.[15] This principle is professionalism.

Modern industrial societies are organized on the basis of a strict social division of labor. There is a wide scope of occupations in any one society. The knowledge required for each is often great. A clear separation has emerged between occupations and also between work per se and leisure. Several strategies have been used to control each occupation's market situation, of which professionalism is one.[16] The chief characteristics derive from those of occupations that were prevalent before or during the process of industrialization, such as medicine and the law. There is, however, much analytic confusion today about the precise nature of professionalism. The main distinction from other occupational strategies appears to be over the producer-consumer relation. In this case, the producer is required to have specialized knowledge and adhere to an ethic of service. Some academics point up distinctions in traits and attributes of professional occupations. For example, one of the early characteristics was given as: ". . . the essence of professionalism . . . is not concerned with self-

interest but with the welfare of the client."[17] From this type of characteriza-
tion, attempts are made to construct a natural history of professions, the more
recent occupations emulating earlier ones by adopting their modes.

The educational profession itself has aroused a strong interest
among researchers. Comparisons are frequently made between the development
of teachers into a profession and that of doctors. One pertinent study tried to
demonstrate that the teachers are merely a 'semi-profession.'[18] This analysis
depended on the assumption of certain universal attributes of all professions.
These have not yet been clearly and convincingly delineated.

In fact, professionalism seems more to be a strong ideal in modern
industrial societies because it is an apparently successful strategy to control
market status. It is thus the model for emergent occupations.[19] It is not
only applicable to the self-employed but also those in bureaucratic organizations.
These kinds of organizations are another central feature of modern industrial
societies. Max Weber, for example, pointed to the close link between the development of professions and bureaucracy.[20] His pessimistic view of the increasing
rationalization of society, characterized by experts with narrow specialisms and
narrowness of vision rather than an ethic of service, was an analysis of both
bureaucratic occupations and professions. It has frequently been used in sub-
sequent analyses, such that Goode asserted: "An industrializing society is a
professionalizing society."[21]

The strategy of professionalism, in sum, is a way of controlling a
work task by collective means and by delineating its boundaries substantively
and ethically. The extent to which an occupation may do this may depend not
only on the nature of the producer-client relationship and client characteristics
but also on organizational context and available resources. The state has, for
example, played a very important part in mediating producer-client relations and
defining the boundaries of certain occupations. Britain provides such an example:
teachers apparently have little control of their situation although they regard
themselves as a profession. The problem has been described thus:

> If we compare the profession of teachers with that of medicine it is
> noticeable, first of all, that the unification which took place in medi-
> cine has been singularly lacking among teachers. The sheer self-
> interest of the State in maintaining control over the profession has
> won out and the likelihood that the teachers will be able to enjoy
> the degree of autonomy and power exercised collectively by the
> medical profession is remote.[22]

Professional control has developed in American education because
full-time administrative staff—namely, superintendents—were appointed to
aid school committees in their decisions on education. Lay citizens could not be
expected to know what was the best educational practice.[23] Administrators

were accorded power to provide information and advice on the direction of the system. Superintendents were a distinctly separate group from teachers within the educational profession. I shall later examine relations between these occupational groups to establish whether the profession is homogeneous. There may well be conflict.[24] This is subsidiary to the general question of the balance between professional and citizen control.

During the early twentieth century much energy went into the development of special skills for these administrators. Training programs, in business management as applied to education, proliferated as education increasingly came to be seen as vital to the economy. As a result, schools began to mirror industrial organizations and developed on a factory model, processing pupils for the labor force.[25]

However, professional control may not apply equally in all areas of educational choice. Professional educators were appointed for their particular expertise, knowledge of the educational rather than the administrative process per se. Citizens may be more reluctant to relinquish control over all decisions on the educational system. In particular, decisions on spending on education, i.e., the budgetary process, may well not be regarded as esoteric problems, thus not requiring professional expertise.[26]

CHOICE OF THE BUDGET

The budget has been chosen as a critical case to demonstrate the extent of citizen, and to examine its obverse, professional control in education. It is ostensibly the least technical set of decisions that have to be taken to run the educational system. It is also an area that can perhaps be regarded as most interesting to citizens since it concerns how their money is allocated to the system. If citizen control is not apparent over the decisions on the budget, it is hardly likely that control would be sustained for issues that are less salient to the community.

Other writers have pointed to budgetary decisions as being most susceptible to citizen control. Kirst made the point simply: "A likely area for community influence would be the general program or salary aspects of the school budget."[27] Certainly it is an area to which elected members may believe they can contribute. Barber and Wildavsky, writing about decision-making not in education but in local government, also commented on the budget as an area of continual citizen interest.[28] Barber added:

> Government officials at all levels eventually come to recognize that pervading power in all its myriad forms, shaping large and small decisions, stimulating here and depressing there reflecting the past power structure and determining that of the future, there is one common element—money![29]

This thesis of professional control fits in with the existing evidence on the government of the American educational system.

THE EXISTING EVIDENCE

This suggests that there is a discrepancy between belief in local democracy and behavior in America, and that the overall modus operandi tends in favor of professional rather then lay control. The academic evidence is not conclusive, but case studies of educational decision-making point up the role of professional educators in suburbia, new towns, small towns, and large cities.[30] They also point out variations in professional control according to political culture. McCarty and Ramsey sought to synthesize this work by developing a typology of professional behavior on the basis of community characteristics and inter-action.[31] This did not relate behavior to types of decisions but asserted administrative strategies as a function only of the characteristics of the local community. The general view that does emerge is that there is some professional control in local communities even though its exact form has not been delineated.

Research studies on large cities, to demonstrate the necessity of community control, showed that the school boards through their small size were not representative of all minority groups and were thus of questionable legitimacy.[32] Secondly, the studies showed that the professional educators had hegemony over the processes of decision-making; that the educational system was closed and not open to the participation and influence of lay citizens. Even after the decentralization of New York City, as a result of community action, the problem of professional control remained, albeit that the bureaucracy rather then the superintendent himself was in control.[33]

The findings about the government of education tie in with evidence about the workings of the political system in general. Political science studies have pointed out that the majority of citizens show little interest in participatory democracy: they neither vote nor involve themselves in local issues.[34] Case studies of individual communities have indicated the pervasive influence of a small elite or special, competing groups rather than a mass of citizens.[35]

It seems that there is an overall modus vivendi which tends towards a closed system, with professional rather than lay control either by citizens or their elected representatives. There appears to be an implicit set of rules which guides the behavior of professional administrators and citizens, beyond the vague notion that professionals attend to administration and elected citizens to policy. The unwritten rules circumscribe the interventions that the citizens may make in the arena of educational decision-making, and they lead to passive behavior on the part of the elected members. Rather than initiating issues with the professional educators, the representatives wait for issues to be brought to their attention and then they react to them. There are two assumptions on which the rules are based. One is that the management of the educational system should rest with the professional educators who are trained experts. They will be able to recognize issues worthy of lay attention. The second is that it is not a legitimate notion of representation that elected members sound out local opinion and initiate change. The situation appears to be as Kerr has asserted:

> School boards chiefly perform the function of legitimising the policies of the school system to the community rather than representing various segments of the community to the school administration, especially with regard to education programs.[36]

Yet this is not necessarily true over all decisions. It may well depend upon the nature of the issues. The evidence accumulated relates only to matters of educational policy or other substantive, political issues. The professional educators may not have the means to control the system in areas where the decisions are not regarded as requiring expert knowledge. In such decisions the influence of professional educators may be circumscribed. Certainly the advocates of community control assumed that participation essentially should be over relevant decisions such as spending on education.[37] Thus there may not be a "zero-sum" model of professional control. Professional influence may relate only to topics needing knowledge of academic practice. Martin and Minar have both shown that citizens show continual interest in financial issues in education.[38]

In sum, the purpose of this book is to examine the extent of citizen participation in a critical case of social policy, which prima facie, offers considerable opportunities for it; namely the American school budgetary process. It will be argued that professional control of this process tends to emerge regardless of such variables as form of government or size of community. This conclusion is of great relevance for evaluating the possibilities of citizen participation in other social policy contexts. It would also seem to apply, a fortiori, to other education systems such as that in Britain, which display less formal concern for community control.[39]

OUTLINE OF THE BOOK

In Chapter 2 the design of the research study to analyze the budgetary process is presented. In Chapter 3 the salient characteristics—social, political, and budgetary—of the four school districts are given. In Chapter 4 an analysis of preparations of the operating budget is presented to set the scene for citizens' deliberations. In Chapter 5 school committees' deliberations on the operating budget as a distinct process are characterized as reactions to the professional educators. The impact of size of school district on school committee behavior is assessed. In Chapter 6 analysis is extended to the involvement of the community. In Chapter 7 salary negotiations are evaluated in terms of citizen or professional control, particularly that of occupational groups within the educational profession. An estimate of the consensus between members of the education profession is made. Chapter 8 is a discussion of whether particular forms of government machinery have an impact upon lay, or representative, citizen participation in the budget and in specific kinds of decisions. Chapter 9 summarizes the argument of the earlier chapters and draws conclusions about the nature and implications of professional control in education.

NOTES TO CHAPTER ONE

1. For details of the reforms see P. Marris and M. Rein, *Dilemmas of Social Reform,* 2nd edition (London; Pelican, 1974) or D.P. Moynihan, *Maximum Feasible Misunderstanding* (New York: Free Press, 1969).
2. See particularly A.A. Altshuler *Community Control* (New York: Pegasus, 1970), Ch. 2.
3. Moynihan, *op. cit.,* and Francis Fox Piven and R.A. Cloward, *Regulating the Poor* (New York: Vintage Books, 1971), ch. 9 & 10.
4. L.J. Fein, *The Ecology of the Public Schools* (New York: Pegasus, 1971), p. 83.
5. H.M. Levin (ed.), *Community Control of Schools* (New York: Clarion, 1970); see particularly M.D. Fantini, "Community Control and Quality Education in Urban School Systems," pp. 40–76.
6. For a more detailed account see L.J. Cremin, *The Transformation of the School* (New York: Knopf, 1961); B. Bailyn, *Education in the Forming of American Society* (Chapel Hill: University of North Carolina Press, 1960).
7. S. Hays, *Municipal Reform in the Progressive Era - Whose Class Interest?* (Boston: New England Free Press, 1972).
8. J.A. Cronin, *The Control of American Schools* (Boston: Little Brown, 1973).
9. J. Burkhead, *State and Local Taxes for Public Education* (Syracuse: Syracuse University Press, 1963); M.W. Kirst, (ed.), *State, School and Politics* (Lexington, Mass.: D.C. Heath, 1972); N. Masters, *State Politics and Public Schools* (New York: Knopf, 1964).
10. S.K. Bailey and E.K. Mosher, *ESEA* (Syracuse: Syracuse University Press, 1968).
11. For details of the intricacies of methods of state equalization, see J.C. Coons, H. Clune, and S. Sugarman, *Private Wealth and Public Education* (Cambridge: Belknap, 1970), ch. 2 to 4.
12. W. Greenbaum, "Serrano Versus Priest" *Harvard Educational Review* (1972); C. Finn and L. Lenkowsky, "Serrano Versus the People," *Commentary* (1972), pp. 68–72; D.P. Moynihan, "Equalizing Education - In Whose Benefit?" *Public Interest* (1972), pp. 69–89; R. Lekachman, "Schools, Money and Politics: Financing Public Education," *The New Leader* (September, 1972), pp. 7–14.
13. J. Koerner, *Who Controls American Education?* (Boston: Beacon, 1968), p. 118.

14. C. Jencks, "Educational Vouchers," *New Republic* (July 4, 1970).
15. Fein, *op. cit.*, ch. 3.
16. T. Johnson, *Professions and Power* (London: MacMillan, 1972); see particularly ch. 3.
17. T.H. Marshall, *Sociology at the Crossroads* (London: Routledge & Kegan Paul, 1939), pp. 158–159.
18. A. Etzioni, *The Semi-Professions and their Organization* (New York: The Free Press, 1969).
19. Johnson, *op. cit.*
20. M. Weber, *Economy and Society* (New York; The Free Press, 1968); Vol. 3, ch. 11.
21. W.J. Goode, "Encroachment, Charlatanism and the Emerging Profession: Psychology, Sociology and Medicine, *American Sociological Review* (1960), pp. 902–913.
22. N. Parry, "Power, Class and Occupational Strategy," *British Sociological Association Conference* (University of Surrey, April 1973), p. 22.
23. R. Callahan, *Education and the Cult of Efficiency* (Chicago: University of Chicago Press, 1962).
24. A.J. Rosenthal, "Administrator-Teacher Relations - Harmony or Conflict?" *Public Administration Review* (June 1967), pp. 154–161.
25. See, for example, M. Lazerson and D. Cohen, "Education and the Corporate Order," *Socialist Revolution* (March–April 1972), pp. 47–72.
26. R. Martin, et al., *Decisions in Syracuse* (Bloomington: Indiana University Press, 1962).
27. M. Kirst (ed.), *The Politics of Education at Federal, State and Local Levels* (Berkeley: McCutchan, 1970), p. 10.
28. J.D. Barber, *Power in Committees* (Chicago: Rand McNally, 1966): A. Wildavsky, "Leave City Budgeting Alone!" In J. Crecine (ed.), *Financing the Metropolis* (Chicago: Aldine, 1968).
29. Barber, *op. cit.*, p. 33.
30. L. Masotti, *Education and Politics in Suburbia* (Cleveland: Press of the Case Western Reserve University, 1967); H.J. Gans *The Levittowners* (New York: Pantheon, 1967); A. Vidich and J. Bensman, *Small Town in Mass Society* (Princeton: Princeton University Press, 1958); J. Coleman, *Community Conflict* (Glencoe: Free Press, 1957); R. Kimborough, *Political Power and Educational Decision-Making* (Chicago: Rand McNally, 1964); R. Martin, et al., *Decisions in Syracuse* (Bloomington: Indiana University Press, 1962); D. Minar, *Decision-Making in Suburban Communities* (Evanston: Northwestern University, 1966).

For a general summary, see A. Rosenthal (ed.), *Governing Education* (New York: Doubleday, 1968); also R.S. Cahill and S.P. Hencley (eds.), *The Politics of Education in the Local Community* (Danville: Interstate, 1964). M. Kirst (ed.), *The Politics of Education at the Federal, State and Local Levels* (Berkeley: McCuchan, 1970).

Marilyn Gittell, *Participants and Participation* (New York: Praeger,

1967); D. Rogers, *110 Livingston Street* (New York: Vintage Books, 1969); P. Schrag, *Village School Downtown* (Boston: Beacon, 1967); J. Pois, *The School Board Crisis* (Chicago: Aldine, 1964); H.L. Summerfield, *The Neighborhood-Based Politics of Education* (Columbus, Ohio: Merrill, 1971).

31. D. McCarty and J.E. Ramsey, *The School Managers* (Westport, Ct.: Greenwood, 1971); ch. 1.

32. M. Gittell and T.E. Hollander, *Six Demonstration School Districts* (New York: Praeger, 1968); M. Gittell and M. Berube (eds.), *Confrontation at Ocean Hill - Brownsville* (New York: Praeger, 1969), especially conclusions.

33. *Ibid.,* p. 331.

34. See, for example, M. Lipset, *Political Man* (London: Heineman, 1959); G. Almond and S. Verba, *The Civic Culture* (Boston: Little Brown, 1965); R.A. Alford, *Bureaucracy and Participation* (Chicago: Rand McNally, 1969); M. Lipsky, *Protest in City Politics* (Chicago: Rand McNally, 1970); P. Bachrach and M. Baratz, *Power and Poverty: Theory and Practice* (London: Oxford University Press, 1970).

35. The debate on elite or pluralist power in communities mainly took place between A. Dahl, *Who Governs?* (New Haven: Yale University Press, 1957); F. Hunter, *The Community Power Structure* (Chapel Hill: University of North Carolina Press, 1953); C.W. Mills, *The Power Elite* (New York: Free Press, 1958); N. Polsby, *Community Power and Political Theory* (New Haven: Yale University Press, 1963). It is summarized by Bachrach and Baratz, *op. cit.,* ch. 1.

36. N. Kerr, *The School Board as an Agent of Legitimation,* Sociology of Education, Fall 1964 p. 35.

37. Fantini, *op. cit.,* p. 51.
Berube and Gittell, *op. cit.,* p. 333.

38. Martin, *op. cit.*
Minar, *op. cit.*

39. See P. Peterson and P. Kantor, *Partisanship and the Limits of Democratic Theory,* Unpublished paper, University of Chicago, 1970; and M. Locke, *Power and Politics in the School System* (London: Routledge, 1974), ch. 11; or O. Banks, *Sociology of Education* (London: Batsford, 1967), particularly ch. 8.

Chapter Two

The School Budgetary Process:
An Analysis

A particular set of educational decisions is to be investigated—the budget—in order to identify and explain the possible and actual spheres of influence of lay and professional participants. In essence, the concern here is with process, the way in which the social division of labor is practiced, without attempting to resolve how local political power groups affect decision-making.[1] The questions are about daily practice, about the behavior of lay and professional participants to control their situations.

The theme is that the system is closed; that professional educators influence and control local decisions because of the discretion accorded them; that lay or representative citizens exercise little direct influence; that they do not explicitly control the educators although they hold them accountable. In this chapter I describe what is meant by the budgetary process—specifically, a school budget—and how it will be analyzed, including the research design and data collection.

WHAT IS THE BUDGETARY PROCESS?

First, one must establish what a budget is and what purpose it serves. Wildavsky's definition is: "A budget is a document containing words and figures, which proposes expenditures for certain items and purposes."[2] There are several ways to construct a budget: as a plan of action—a statement of future purposes—or as a contract—a set of relationships between participants. It is always oriented to the future, but in practice there may be a difference between plans and achievements. The budget is not a once-and-for-all act. It is a statement for a period of time within an ongoing organization. Past precedents and actions greatly affect statements for the future. For the most part a budget is a reassessment of existing conditions. Proposed changes may be slight, and the budget may be used to confirm actual conditions. Budgets, in fact, usually change little from year to year: it is not common to find substantial annual departures from existing practice. Wildavsky states: "Once enacted the budget becomes precedent; the fact that something has been done before greatly increases the chances that it will be done again."[3] Tyl van Geel pointed to the "ratchet principle" in one of the two school districts that he studied, " . . . which holds that the funding of a standard shall not fall below the level established the previous year."[4]

Budgeting is about allocating resources to certain ends, usually on an annual basis within an organization. Since most organizations pursue many goals and use various resources, budgeting is potentially complex as regards both process and decisions. The common technique for budgeting has been termed "disjointed incrementalism."[5] As Simon points out, choices are not usually for the optimal running of an organization but merely for the satisfactory.[6] He terms the process "satisficing." Since any organization has to continue to function, its commitments to clients and employees cannot readily be reversed. Comparisons are made of the previous appropriations with the existing year for categories of resources. Although this may involve programs, it more often concerns departments of an organization over items of expenditure, with a "line item budget." Changes made to existing circumstances are normally about adaptation rather than innovation. It is rare that "zero-base" reviews are made; that is, consideration of a department or program on its intrinsic merits. Whitehead makes the point that "experience has shown that trying to run an organization or major agency with annual zero-base reviews is impossible."[7] A common technique is to use formulae for recurrent resources such as supplies to cover all the constituent departments, derived from experience. Budget reviewers often only look at totals rather than the component parts of the budget and "eyeball" the changes, bearing in mind circumstances such as inflation.

There is no developed theory of budgeting, although recently there have been many analyses of the budgetary process in the public and private sectors of the economy. As a result of those in the 1960s, new techniques have been proposed to help budget-makers formulate their purposes and actions. Initially they were treated as "ideal" ways of dealing with the issue of choice over expenditures. Later administrators recognized them only as aids in sorting out priorities and determining necessary or discretionary items.[8] New techniques such as PPBS or its variant, program budgeting, have introduced an important new element—the explicit consideration of goals. PPBS is, for example, defined as a process whereby the budgeter: (a) defines the objectives of the organization as clearly as possible; (b) finds out what the money was being spent for and what was being accomplished; (c) defines the alternative policies for the organization for the future and collects as much information as possible about what each would cost and what each would do; and (d) sets up a systematic procedure for bringing the relevant information together at a time when decisions are being made.[9]

There are three aspects. One is making explicit the choices between goals and purposes. Another is defining the process structurally and procedurally. The third crucial component is the continual monitoring of the system and its purposes in line with actual spending. The majority of organizations have not fully implemented PPBS because of this last requirement. School systems in the USA, according to Tyl van Geel, have not done so because of the increasing conflict among participants about educational goals.[10] Yet, as Alice Rivlin states, PPBS, whether or not it is well implemented, has made possible explicit budget decisions.[11] It has ensured a re-evaluation of past decisions in the context of organizational goals. If nothing more, it has introduced a common-sense notion to budgeting.

Changes are made, with or without new techniques, by advocacy or bargaining between participants.[12] Since most organizations pursue a multiplicity of goals that defy specification and are often contradictory, assumptions are usually made about key areas of interest. The new techniques encompass methods of changes, usually over all resources and over a longer period than one year. Old techniques required an annual assessment and perhaps only the effect on the total budget.

The budget relates to proposed expenditures: usually only revenue and not capital. Capital costs are considered separately and may be the responsibility of another set of personnel. Wildavsky and Barber show that government agencies, at the federal and local levels, consider source of revenue separately from budgeting; the latter is the allocation of revenue.[13] I will also confine the study to decisions on resource allocation between educational goals.

WHAT ARE THE COMPONENTS OF THE SCHOOL BUDGET?

"The school budget determines the educational program for the future and establishes priorities and levels of instructional activity."[14] What are the issues within the budget of a school district? A school system is complex, with numerous goals or purposes that relate primarily to elementary and secondary education. Although all children resident in the geographical community are eligible to attend the public schools, not all choose to do so. There is no one principle around which to organize curricula, for they have to serve many purposes and clients. Parents and pupils are but facets of the community. The labor force is another.

The main resource of the education system is personnel, for education is a labor-intensive industry: pupils are taught in small groups by specialist staff members. Decisions on personnel are the most important budget component. Two key issues are (a) decisions on professional and support personnel—numbers and levels—and (b) the remuneration for each category. Salary scales and inflationary increases are now determined through negotiation between the staff and the employers, which are the school committees. Collective bargaining may or may not be thought of as integral to budgeting.[15] Yet the decisions taken have implications for all other resources. The salary bill normally constitutes over 80 percent of the budget.[16]

Second, buildings are vital for the educational system. Plant operation and maintenance, or renewal, is a basic budget consideration. Although school committees are not generally responsible for the cost of new buildings, they have to determine the need for new plant. Whether or not it will be provided is decided in Massachusetts by a separate municipal body. Capital for financing the building is raised through bonds issued by that body. For example, the ordinances of one of the districts studied state:

> The school committee, so far as appropriations are made therefor by the Board's Aldermen shall have full power and authority to furnish all school building with proper fixtures, furnishings and equipment . . . It shall be the original judge of expediency and necessity of having additional or improved accommodation for any public school within the limits of the city.[17]

Servicing the instructional programs is a third vital component of the budget. This relates to supplies and equipment, which may be consumed annually or fixed for a time. It is here that there are possibilities for change, by way of development or deletion of instructional programs. They may be continued because of constraints such as state regulations or college entrance requirements. The fourth issue is the support of services to the instructional programs such as administration, research and development, educational aides, and extracurricula activities such as sports and music.

The basic issues are the organization of the educational system over instructional programs, their staffing through the pupil-teacher ratio, and their building and administrative supports. Most important are salaries. The budget can be approached in various ways, for there are few fixed items from outside. The state does not stipulate but it may suggest certain programs such as elementary lunch or special education.[18] To obtain more state financing, the district may have to maintain building standards and some earmarked programs. In 1972, for example, the states required their districts to adopt the federally aided elementary lunch program. The state may also impose constraints such as over collective bargaining and actual personnel contracts. Local laws often pertain about the types and levels of personnel. The school district, however, is free to choose curricula, staff, and remuneration.

The school budgetary process may be extensive, evaluating the system in terms of its goals. Or it may be brief, merely ensuring the system's smooth running as a continuous activity from one year to the next. It is this very scope on which I will focus in order to identify participant involvements.

THE ANALYSIS OF THE SCHOOL BUDGETARY PROCESS

Although past precedents greatly condition what budget changes can be made in any one year, one budgetary cycle is taken as the basis of this study. This period covers the initial deliberations to final decisions on appropriations, but not those about available revenue. These may be closely intertwined, and indeed, increases on the tax rate may be seen as a critical constraint on the process.[19] Concern lies not with the execution and implementation of budget decisions, but with decisions made to retain the status quo or to change the system by additions or deletions of programs or personnel.

The definition of the process and its breadth by the school district itself is used. Changes may not be construed as budget decisions by the participants. This definition is important in order to establish spheres of influence because the analysis is predicated on the dynamic interaction between perceptions and actual behavior by participants.

Since budgeting is an annual event, a detailed scrutiny of relations in one year would reveal the kinds of participant influence. The participants may be divided into two main categories. First are the professional educators, the producers of the system. The term defies simple definition, for it relates not only to the administrators—the superintendent and his office team—but also to the school personnel—principals and teachers.[20] They may not be a homogeneous group. The second category is the community. The elected members on the school committee and other politicians such as financial and other municipal officials are the main consumers. There are also interest groups who may act separately and independently as consumers: parents, pupils, and political pressure groups.

The aim of the analysis is to establish whether the system is usually open, that is, whether lay citizens are provided with, and use, opportunities to participate and contribute to deliberations on budget changes. The obverse is a closed system in which decisions are taken by the elected and appointed officials alone. Interest articulation would then be made by either the producers alone or the elected officials on behalf of the lay citizens.

Thus the analysis will be concerned with both the machinery and use of it by sets of participants. It will also establish attitudes towards its efficacy. Although one year of the budget cycle is the basis, a brief review of the process and relations in previous years is made. However, an assumption was made that if relations for all schools districts are similar, the process would be the same over time.

Alternate Approaches

Obviously other methods could have been chosen. First it may be more useful to look at relations through episodic rather than perennial issues.[21] Financial crises may have more clearly revealed parts played by participants on occasion, and adduced more evidence of citizen influence. In any one year the community may be satisfied with the instructional programs and not involve themselves in the decision process. Or decisions may be negative, that is, be nondecisions, and only take effect slowly and over a long time. However, my interest is in the "normal" spheres of influence rather than in exceptional circumstances. Martin showed that in suburban communities continued citizen interest lay in financial issues and not in educational policy.[22] One year could, of course, be too short a time for this interest to surface, but is unlikely, given the overtly nonspecialist nature of financial decisions.

Another approach to the problem would have been to study a large number of school districts by means of a statistical survey analysis, to make generalizations about the control of the American education system. Statistical studies, such as those of Gittell and James, have been undertaken on large American cities.[23] Neither of these studies addressed the issue of the relationship between behavior and attitudes but instead focussed on the actual expenditures of the school districts under study. The variables of interest in this study are not easily subject to quantification. They are the actions and attitudes of a relatively unknown set of participants over time. The important issues are the everyday conceptions of the situation and the actual behavior that occurs. The point is to understand both the attitudes towards the process and the interaction between those attitudes and the behavior that is observed.

The Chosen Budget Cycle

The cycle studied consisted of the preparations and deliberations for the 1973 budget in Massachusetts. This budget year was, in fact, unusual and could therefore yield evidence both of a perennial issue and an episodic or crisis situation.

In 1972 all school districts in Massachusetts had to prepare budgets for a period of 18 months rather than the usual 12 months. (Although school districts in Massachusetts have fiscal autonomy they are still, legally, agents of the state.) The Massachusetts State Legislature in 1969 passed chapter 849 of the State Laws to change budgets from a calendar to a national fiscal year cycle. Chapter 766 of the Acts of 1971 set January 1st, 1973, to June 30th, 1974, as the 18-month transitional period. One 18-month budget was chosen to achieve the change speedily.

One reason for the fiscal change was that it was customary for municipalities to finalize proposed expenditures by April 1st of the year of effect, three months after the beginning of the financial year. For three months of the budget year, there inevitably was limited and yet speculative spending. A second reason is that the federal fiscal year differed from the state's and its localities. Yet they have a fiscal relationship with federal government, which was complicated by two separate cycles. The new cycle would be more appropriate to school districts for a third reason: the fiscal and academic school year would be almost synonymous. The process of estimating expenditures would be simpler. For example, contracts for teachers are usually negotiated for the academic year so that one contract would suffice in the new budget. Formerly a budget generally consisted of two contracts with the professional employees, one for the remaining academic year and a new one for the year starting in the fall. In recent years the new contracts could not be settled before the statutory deadline due to increased teacher militancy, making budgeting difficult.[24]

The 18-month budget would involve the school districts in explicating their priorities because of the effect upon the tax rate. The intention was to set one tax rate. It might look much larger than one for 12 months. Indeed, it might actually be larger than one for 50 percent more. In the case of education, the additional period would include more for salaries through new contract negotiations. It would also have to cover two winters when more school activities habitually take place. In particular, plant operation and maintenance is more costly especially because of heating. A school year is usually assumed to be 10 rather than 12 months. Teachers are paid for 10 months' work, to cover a two-month vacation. Vacation pay may be included optionally in the monthly salary. The additional six months' costs would be greater than half of the school year. An 18-month budget was certainly both an unusual and a habitual event.

THE CHOICE OF SCHOOL DISTRICTS

Since participant interaction was likely to be complex and covered almost a year, I chose only four school districts, all in Massachusetts. Size and government machinery were the two variables used in selection to provide the data of organizational effects on professional control and its obverse citizen participation. There is little empirical evidence of variation in professional or citizen influences on these dimensions. Differences are usually attributed to community characteristics such as political culture or wealth.[25] Yet the rhetoric of community control proclaimed that the large size of a district was inimical to citizen participation.[26] Evidence, such as that of Peterson for Britain and Hamilton for USA shows machinery to have an effect in actual participation.[27] The main issues to be examined, then, are that the more machinery as formal opportunities for citizen participation and the smaller the school district, the greater the extent of citizen involvement and influence over annual budgetary decisions.

Government Machinery

The ways in which democratic principles are translated into practice are likely to affect participation by the representative or lay citizens. The essence of any democratic organization is to afford citizens opportunities to contribute opinion and information on its workings.[28] This is also the case for budgetary decisions. Actual practice may vary with implications for professional or lay control. There are at least three criteria of democratic machinery for education in America.[29] One is the electoral process; second are fiscal arrangements; and third is the form of government machinery. Through the electoral process citizens express their opinions about the running of the educational system by choosing between candidates of partisan or non-partisan persuasion. In Massachusetts, all school boards have to be chosen on a non-partisan basis. The only variations between districts are the number of members (around seven) and the length of time they stay in office (around 3 to 4 years). Thus variation in participation of lay or elected citizens here may be limited only by the idiosyncracies of the individual candidates.

Fiscal differences arise from the various methods of raising educational revenue. The basic mechanism is the tax rate, but it may be operated in two ways.[30] One is *fiscal dependence*. School boards have to submit proposed budgets to the municipal officials who have the legal right to alter appropriations. Since school boards cannot raise revenue they are inevitably subject to municipal control. This may amount to nothing more than an interest in the total budget size. On the other hand, it may mean official or lay influence over instructional programs. Kirst states:

> Typically the mayor in fiscally independent or dependent cities does not become involved in the program decisions of the budget. The mayor restricts the area of influence to the overall budget ceiling the tax base can stand . . . a way to accumulate more influence for increased taxes may be to surrender some influence over curricula . . . to non-school groups that will support higher taxes.[31]

The second is *fiscal autonomy* or independence. This reflects the traditional ideology that education should be above machine and partisan politics.[32] Schools boards again do not have the power to raise revenue but must obtain their finances from the local property tax. The municipal officials have no legal power to challenge the school committee budget proposals. They must automatically raise the amount that is requested annually. These arrangements may have very little differential effect on budget outcomes, although they do affect procedures of decision-making and interactions.[33] In any event, fiscal autonomy prevails in Massachusetts even though constant threats are made to change the system.

Form of Government Machinery

Two forms of general municipal machinery exist in Massachusetts— town and city. The predominant form, as in most of New England, is the *town*. It involves a very old principle of democracy, that of citizen assembly for decisions. The town meeting, the focus of the town's political activity, is an annual event to decide revenue, capital expenditures and substantive policies. Within the town form are those applying the mode of direct citizen assembly— any citizen is eligible to attend the meeting. The others use a form of representative citizen assembly, where precincts elect citizens as town meeting members.

In the *city,* the principle is representative democracy, government by an elected mayor and aldermen or councillors. In some cities the mayor is vested with powers which extend over every city committee, including schools. In others the mayor has a weaker legal position, with that of the city council or aldermen commensurately stronger. Both bodies are nevertheless responsible for raising the city's finances through the tax rate.

Gross has shown that within fiscally independent systems different government machinery does have some independent effect upon procedures. All work in the direction of exerting pressure on professional educators and committees.[34] Two towns and two cities were chosen to investigate the impact on budget participation of this machinery. Formally it is very different. The towns ostensibly allow for extensive lay participation and involvement. The cities allow only involvement by representatives of the community. The presumption is that in the towns there would be more citizen participation and less professional control than in the cities. The towns studied are Weston and Wellesley; the cities, Melrose and Quincy.

Size

The other crucial variable is community size on the assumption that the smaller the community, the greater the likelihood of citizen participation. This notion is derived from the community control literature.[35] It is that in smaller communities citizens are closer and able to have more contact with the system. Closeness could provide citizens with an incentive to participate. The smaller the system, the less likely it can sustain a large educational bureaucracy unresponsive to its citizens. A larger system may contain a demographically heterogeneous population. There is more possibility of value conflicts between parents, other citizens, and elected representatives. I chose to select communities other than very large cities. Evidence exists of the lack of participation there. I chose to concentrate on communities which possibly exhibited a different pattern, and ones which the city advocates of community control wished to emulate.

The choice of actual district was conditioned by the variable of government machinery and the fact that there is municipal variation in educational provision. Of the 351 Massachusetts municipalities, only 150 provide both elementary and secondary education.[36] On the other hand, only one city merited exclusion on the grounds of being a large city—Boston.

The smallest district was therefore chosen by reference to its overall

Table 2-1. Population Sizes of the Municipalities

Municipality	Population 1970*	Public School Population 1971**
Weston	10,070	2,853
Wellesley	28,051	5,902
Melrose	33,180	7,556
Quincy	87,966	16,735

*Source: Federal census.
**Source: Massachusetts Department of Education, Annual Statistics compiled from school districts.

population and public school enrollment. Weston was selected as a town with a public school enrollment of 2,853 and a total population of 10,070, according to 1971 statistics. For comparison with the other municipalities, see Table 2-1. I chose next a town that was large by comparison with Weston but would also compare well with a small city. Wellesley was therefore chosen as a large town with a population of 28,051 and a public school enrollment of 5,902 as of 1971. Very small cities are few in number and the main range is around 30,000 in total population. Melrose was chosen with a total population of 33,180 and a public school enrollment of 7,556 in 1971. Finally I chose one larger city to compare with the others. It is not large by national standards, and ranks eleventh in Massachusetts. The city is Quincy. Its overall population was 87,966 in 1970, and its public school enrollment 16,735.

Controlling for other Variables

In choosing districts, an attempt was made to control for variables which might have a mediating effect upon citizen participation, such as wealth and other municipal activities.[37] Education, indeed, does not constitute the sole municipal service. In the smaller areas the municipality usually has fewer legal responsibilities for services: education is a larger proportion of the budget. Yet in all districts education is the largest single budget item, as shown in Table 2-2. More importantly, the wealth of a district as measured by its property valuations or citizens' socioeconomic circumstances influence budget considerations.[38] Table 2-3 shows equalized property valuations. This in itself is neither a sufficient measure of circumstance nor the citizens' evaluation of the importance of education. Revenue available through the tax base, which is one indication of wealth, may have an impact at two levels. First that will affect the absolute amount that the community is willing to spend on education. James found that:

> The financial resources of a community and the character of its population are major determinants of that community's educational policy: they set boundaries beyond which we should not expect the

Table 2-2. Municipal Tax Rates

Municipality	Percent for Public Schools*	Equalized School*	School**	General**	Total**
		Tax Rates (per $1,000) in 1971			
Weston	62	20.9	21	13	34
Wellesley	54	22.7	26	22	48
Melrose	47	19.9	20	23	43
Quincy	41	26.9	58	84	142

*Source: Massachusetts Teachers Association Research Bulletin No. 712-9.
**Source: Massachusetts Department of Education.

decision-making behavior of governmental officials, and the influence of governmental arrangements themselves, to reach.[39]

Secondly it will affect content of budget discussions. According to the available evidence, in the poor districts controversy is likely over basic spending, and in the very wealthy but heterogeneous populations, differences will arise over "educational frills."[40] I tried to control for financial circumstances to evaluate independently the effects of government machinery and size. I used educational spending as an indicator of socioeconomic circumstances and educational interest.

It was not possible to choose four communities with exactly the same expenditure. I chose within form of government. Table 2-4 shows that the two towns and two cities both have similar levels of spending. There may, in fact, still be differences in the absolute wealth measured by tax base, which may lead to variant political cultures, but expenditure probably indicates similar attitudes to education.

The main issues are the effects of absolute size and government machinery on citizen participation and professional control. The four school districts may be classified on these two dimensions, as shown in Table 2-5.

Table 2-3. Municipal Property Valuations

Municipality	Equalized Property Valuations Per Child* 1969-70
Weston	$36,925
Wellesley	$42,194
Melrose	$23,331
Quincy	$24,029

*The figure is derived by dividing equalized valuations by number of school attending children.
Source: Massachusetts Teachers Association Research Bulletin No. 712-9.

Table 2-4. School Expenditures

Municipality	Per Pupil Cost 1970-1
Weston	$1,438
Wellesley	$1,264
Melrose	$ 868
Quincy	$ 919

Source: Massachusetts Teachers Association Research Bulletin No. 712-9, Part 1.

Table 2-5. The School District by the Key Variables

	Size	
Form of Government	Large	Small
Town	Wellesley	Weston
City	Quincy	Melrose

MEASURES OF PARTICIPATION
AND INFLUENCE

This study is exploratory. I do not use elaborate measures of participation or influence. I rely on crude indications of the range of participants and measures of their spheres of influence in the process and outcomes of the budget. I do not assume a zero-sum model of decision-making, that only one set of participants— either the professional educators, elected or lay citizens—can influence decisions. I expect their contributions in various spheres, such as educational, technical, or political matters, or financial costs alone as over the total budget.

   To determine critical influence of, and therefore control by, participants, I examine both available formal opportunities, such as meetings, as well as their actual use in terms of time spent and content. I also look at informal interaction and contact between sets of participants and individuals. The final criterion of influence is the effect on decisions about future appropriations for expenditure. Since salaries constitute the largest proportion of the budget total—about 80 percent as Table 2-6 shows—I confine the analysis to changes in outcome to the budget totals or components such as program deletions or the adoption of a new instructional program. I do not concentrate on decisions about the reallocation of resources.

   There are two basic areas of investigation: the division of labor between the participants and the procedural mode of decision-making. The division of labor is essentially between four sets of participants, usually professional educators, members of the school committee, municipal officials, and lay citizens. What contribution does each set of participants make to substantive decisions and how extensive is it?

Table 2-6. **Salary Proportions in School Budgets**

Municipality	1972
Weston	76%
Wellesley	76%
Melrose	89.65%
Quincy	82%

Source: Data provided by superintendents.

      The mode of decision-making is used as a way of looking at the type of relations between participants. It is taken to cover the procedures for making substantive decisions and involving groups in the process. It is a secondary illustration of spheres of influence.

      Further, the whole budgetary process is divided into three parts to measure these two aspects to deliberations. The idea is derived from James' analysis of the budgetary process in 14 large cities.[42] James divided the process into two main stages as a way of distinguishing between types and levels of decision. They are the process of preparation and that of determination. The *process of preparation* refers to the stage at which the elements of the budget are put together and the necessary resources evaluted. Typically this is handled by the professional educators, but there may be informal opportunities for citizens and the municipal officials to contribute and set the tone for the actual decisions. The *process of determination* refers to that stage when the elected officials are ostensibly in ascendance. It covers deliberations on formulated budget proposals. This is the key to understanding interaction and actual budget refinements. However, it is conditioned by the previous activities. In this study this is not sufficient. Because of the dissonance in annual scheduling of the operating budget and salary negotiations and because of changes in the formality of negotiations, these two processes are distinct. As one school superintendent said: "Salary negotiations is [*sic*] an integral but separate part of the budget building process."[43] Thus, salary negotiations are treated separately, and processes of preparation and determination refer only to parts of the operating budgets.

RESEARCH METHODS

The data on which this analysis is based are drawn from three basic sources: participant observation of budget meetings; interviews with the key participants, and scrutiny of the reports of the school departments. The first source was the direct observation of the process for the operating budget. I attended meetings of professional educators and those whom they chose to involve in preparations. I also observed the meetings held in public to deliberate on the budget proposed by school committees. This included school committee meetings both with the professional educators and municipal officials. Whenever possible, I also attended the executive sessions of the school committees.

Secondly I conducted structured, open-ended interviews with the key officials—26 school committee members, 3 municipal officials and professional educators, being 4 superintendents, and 18 administrators and principals, and 4 teachers' representatives. No systematic interviews were conducted with lay citizens, although informal discussions were held with local newspaper reporters and representatives of the League of Women Voters.

Thirdly I inspected the internal and newspaper reports of the school districts' budgetary activities over the past five years.

The analysis relied on a mixture of research techniques because of the lack of specificity of the dependent variables and the wish to establish the interaction between attitudes and observed behavior. In fact, the interviews are used as confirmations of observations and to elicit attitudes to involvements in the process as well as factual material that was impossible to collect by direct observation.[44]

SUMMARY

Budgeting has been shown to be a lengthy and complex process even in the area of school decisions. It covers issues such as the direction of the school system as well as the allocation of resources for specific purposes. Therefore, a one-year cycle has been chosen for study. The basic question is the extent to which professional educators critically influence the educational process, particularly financial decisions. The study seeks to determine the boundaries of that influence in four different settings, on the premise that there will be differences according to size and form of government machinery of the community. The actual contributions from lay citizens may be such that this thesis of professional control cannot be sustained for Quincy, Melrose, Wellesley, and Weston.

NOTES TO CHAPTER TWO

1. There have been many studies concerned with the locus of power, either within the local school district or in the state. For the best summaries see: M. Kirst (ed.), *State, School and Politics* (Lexington, Mass.: D.C. Heath, 1972); or L. Iannaconne and F.W. Lutz, *Politics, Power and Policy: The Governing of Local School Districts.* (Columbus, Ohio: Merrill, 1970); or A. Rosenthal (ed.), *Governing Education* (Garden City: Doubleday, 1969).

2. A. Wildavsky, *The Politics of the Budgetary Process.* (Boston: Little, Brown, 1964), p. 7.

3. *Ibid.,* p. 9.

4. Tyl Van Geel, *Efficiency, Effectiveness in Local School Systems.* Unpublished

doctoral dissertation, Harvard Graduate School of Education,: 1972, p. 246.

5. D. Braybrooke and C. Lindblom, *A Strategy of Decision* (New York: Free Press, 1963), ch. 3.

6. H.A. Simon, *Administrative Behavior* (New York: MacMillan, 1959).

7. C. Whitehead, *The Uses and Limitations of Systems Analysis* (Santa Monica, Ca.: Rand, 1967), p. 32.

8. C. Schultze, *The Politics and Economics of Public Spending* (Washington D.C.: Brookings Institution, 1968).

9. C. Whitehead, *op. cit.,* p. 18.

10. Geel, *op. cit.,* conclusions.

11. Alice Rivlin, *Systematic Thinking for Social Action* (Washington, D.C.: Brookings Institution, 1971) introduction.

12. C. Lindblom, "The Science of Muddling Through," *Public Administration Review* (1952), pp. 79–88; or A. Wildavsky, *op. cit.,* conclusions.

13. *Ibid;* J.D. Barber, *Power in Committees* (Chicago: Rand McNally, 1966).

14. M. Kirst, *The Politics of Education at the Federal, State and Local Levels* (Berkeley, Ca.: McCutchan, 1970), p. 6.

15. H.T. James, James A. Kelly and Walter I. Garms, *The School Budget Process in Large Cities.* In A. Rosenthal (ed.), *Governing Education* (Garden City: Doubleday, 1969), pp. 314–341.

16. *Ibid.*

17. *Melrose City Ordinances,* revised 1956, Title 5, sections 33 and 34.

18. M. Kirst and F. Wirt, *The Political Web of American Schools* (Boston: Little Brown, 1972), ch. 3.

19. W. Bloomberg and M. Sunshine, *Suburban Power Structures and Public Education: A Study of Values, Influence and Tax Effort* (Syracuse: Syracuse University Press, 1963).

20. See, for example, M. Gittell, *Participants and Participation* (New York: Praeger, 1966), introduction, pp. 46, 48, & 54.

21. Roscoe Martin, et al., *Government and the Suburban School* (Syracuse: Syracuse University Press, 1962), p. 12.

22. *Ibid.*

23. M. Gittell and T.E. Hollander *Six Demonstration School Districts* (New York: Praeger, 1969); H.T. James, *op. cit.*

24. C.R. Perry and W.A. Wildman, *The Impact of Negotiations on Public Education* (Worthington, Ohio: Jones, 1970); or A. Rosenthal, *Pedagogues and Power: Teacher Groups in School Politics* (Syracuse University Press, 1969).

25. See M. Kirst and M. Wirt, *op. cit.,* ch. 4.

26. See, for example, M. Berube and M. Gittell, *The Confrontation at Oceanhill - Brownsville* (New York: Praeger, 1969), conclusions and epilogue.

27. P. Peterson and P. Kantor, *Partisanship and the Limits of Democratic Theory.* Unpublished paper, University of Chicago, 1970. S.H. Hamilton, *Class & Politics in the USA* (New York: Wiley 1972).

28. R.A. Dahl, *Preface to Democratic Theory* (Chicago: Chicago University Press, 1956) ch. 5.

29. R.A. Dahl, *Who Governs?* (New Haven: Yale University Press, 1961), p. 314.
30. Jesse Burkehead, *State and Local Taxes for Public Education* (Syracuse: Syracuse University Press, 1963): or J. Cronin, *The Control of American Schools* (Boston: Little Brown, 1972), pp. 22–25.
31. Kirst, *op. cit.,* pp. 7 & 12.
32. J. Cronin, *op. cit.,* ch. 2.
33. See N. Gross, *Who Controls Our Schools?* (New York: Wiley, 1958), p. 53.
34. *Ibid,* p. 53; N. Gross, *Explorations in Role Analysis* (New York: Wiley, 1958), ch. 15.
35. Berube and Gittell, *op. cit.,* conclusions.
36. Information from Mass. Department of Commerce and Development.
37. Bloomberg, *op. cit.*
38. H. Thomas James, James A. Kelly, and Walter I. Garms, *Determinants of Educational Expenditures in Large Cities of the United States* U.S. Dept. of Health, Education & Welfare, Office of Education. Cooperative Research Project No. 2389 (Stanford, Calif. School of Education, Stanford University, 1966) p. 32.
39. *Ibid.*
40. L.J. Fein, *The Ecology of Public Schools* (New York: Pegasus, 1971), ch. 3.
41. James, *op. cit.*
42. Interview with Dr. L. Creedon, Quincy, Massachusetts, in February 1973.
43. C. Argyris, *Intervention Theory and Method* (Reading, Mass.: Addison, Wesley, 1970) inspired this.

Chapter Three

Four School Districts: A Portrait

Budgeting takes place within a social and political context. The four school districts have been selected to compare in size and form of government machinery. They are standardized by school spending as a proxy for wealth, socioeconomic characteristics, and educational interest. They could also vary in other ways. What are the similarities and differences between them? Who are the citizens who live there? In this chapter I depict the four school districts, specifically in the winter of 1972-3, to set the scene for the budget analysis.

SOCIAL HISTORIES AND CIRCUMSTANCES

The four school districts are alike in that they are all suburban areas to Boston, almost equidistant from the center of Commonwealth. Here likeness ends. Quincy, the larger city, is not only a residential community but also supports several flourishing industries, particularly the quarrying of granite and ship-yards which are important to the American economy.[1] The city is described as follows:

> Today Quincy is primarily a manufacturing city although the extent of its retail trade also establishes it as an area shopping center. In 1970 a total of 1447 firms [were] reported. . . .[2]

Although it is located south of Boston on the ocean and has 27 miles of coast-line, it is not a resort. The summer houses have, in recent years, been converted to year-round residences.

Melrose, the smaller city, is predominantly residential. Only 4,000 persons were registered as employed within the city in 1970, in 396 firms.[3] Its citizens mostly commute to work in and around Boston.

The two towns are more similar to Melrose than to Quincy. Both are basically residential communities. Wellesley, however, is increasingly supporting industries, mainly service or commercial. Its proportion of internal employees was higher than that in Melrose in 1970: 7,339 persons in 617 firms.[4] Weston is clearly only a dormitory suburb. Only 6 firms reported to the Division of Employment Security in 1970, employing an average of 48 persons.[5]

The communities have developed thus because of their unique histories. Quincy is one of the oldest communities in the Commonwealth, originally settled in 1625. It produced two of the early presidents, John Adams and John Quincy Adams. By the nineteenth century it had been incorporated as a town, and on May 17th, 1888, it became a city. By the turn of the century it was well established as a thriving industrial and residential community. Its growth in this century has been relatively stable, and by the late 1960s its population—especially in the schools—was slowly declining, and aging.[6]

Wellesley also has claims to American history. It was settled in the seventeenth century, but incorporated in 1711 as part of the town of Needham. It became an independent town in 1881, and already possessed "a shoddy mill, shoe factory and paint factory and chemical plant," largely employing the local Italian citizens.[7] It had established a strong reputation because Wellesley College, one of the major female seminaries in the country, was founded there in 1871. The school became quickly renowned and therefore influenced the character of the town. Other schools were founded in its wake. The town has grown fivefold since the turn of the century, but its pace of growth slowed in the 1960s. It is still a popular area to live because of its natural beauty, and a majority of residents remain past retirement. It has been cited as one of the few very attractive "safe places" to live in America.[8]

Melrose is also an old community, incorporated in the nineteenth century first as a town in 1850 and later in 1899, as a city. Prior to that it was politically active. Goss states that as early as 1691 "town records show that action was taken for the education of children. . . .[and] in 1712 a building was erected for the purpose. . . ."[9] Its growth in the twentieth century has been less marked, having only doubled in size. In the 1960s the rate of growth accelerated.

Weston is the most modern of the four districts. It was originally settled as an agricultural community in 1713 where "emphasis was placed on the raising of fruit and vegetables."[10] Its main development has been in the twentieth century, doubling in size from 1950 to 1970. Its growth was considerable in the 1960s.

The citizens of the four districts are now rather different, although all are ethnically homogeneous, mainly of WASP or Italian or Irish Catholic origin. Quincy contains a wide occupational mix, with a large proportion in clerical, craft, and operative jobs. Indeed, its median income in 1960 of $6,785 was below the average for the Boston metropolitan area.[12] Less than 20 percent had incomes over $10,000.[13] Comparisons are shown in Tables 3-1,

Table 3-1. Occupational Classifications, 1960

| | *Percentage of Total in:* | | | |
	Quincy	*Melrose*	*Wellesley*	*Weston*
Professional, Technical	12.5	18.7	23.6	25.5
Managers, etc.	8.4	12.0	19.6	23.9
Clerical, etc.	21.4	19.8	14.8	11.9
Sales	9.2	10.1	12.9	10.7
Craft, Foreman	17.0	14.7	6.4	4.4
Operatives	14.1	11.7	4.4	4.4
Service	8.1	6.1	6.8	5.2

Source: The U.S. population census: reported by Mass. Department of Commerce and Development.

3-2, and 3-3. Weston provides the greatest contrast since most of its residents pursue professional or managerial jobs. Over two-thirds of those employed had incomes over $10,000 in 1960, the median being $13,703.[14] Wellesley's residents also are in predominantly professional or managerial jobs, with incomes generally well above $10,000 and around a median of $11,478 in 1960.[15] Melrose's citizens are rather more evenly spread over the occupational spectrum, with just over a quarter of the occupied having incomes above $10,000, and around a median of $7,507 in 1960.[16]

POLITICAL ATTRIBUTES

Inevitably these socioeconomic circumstances affect political attitudes. Quincy indeed has had a majority of registered Democrats (see Table 3-4), although the tendency has been to elect Republican mayors. The mayor elected in 1971 was a Republican and had served as a state representative.[17] This election showed the swing back toward political conservatism which has arisen slowly in local politics during the last decade. Is this a result, perhaps, of a declining and aging community? It has several manifestations: in particular, a strong pressure group to counter inflation by means of censuring local tax increases was established. The Quincy Taxpayers Revolt was very vociferous, frequently publicizing their news over the two local newspapers and radio station. Gaining influence in local policy decisions, the Revolt has succeeded in preventing or delaying new school building in recent years. Though it has not yet supported

Table 3-2. Median Family Incomes, 1960

Quincy	*Melrose*	*Wellesley*	*Weston*
$6,785	$7,507	$11,478	$13,703

Source: The U.S. population census: reported by Mass. Department of Commerce and Development.

Table 3-3. Family Income Distribution, 1960

Proportion over $10,000			
Quincy	Melrose	Wellesley	Weston
19.0	26.6	57.3	68.6

Note: The Boston metropolitan area average is 21.37.
Source: The U.S. population census: reported by Mass. Department of Commerce and Development.

candidates for political office, it has achieved its aim of ensuring that representatives were "fiscally responsible."

By 1972, Quincy was a volatile community in an area which had always been active and where obtaining political office has been particularly arduous. Moreover, types of political office has been extended to include school committee membership, which previously had been viewed as a civic duty for parents with children currently in school or for those particularly interested in education per se. In the election of 1971 there were 23 candidates for three seats, indicating considerable local political interest. The newly elected three of the six-member team were political activists, holding this office as a step toward a wider political career. Two were recently married lawyers in their twenties. The other three members consisted of two long-standing, basically interested educationists, although one had recently joined the Taxpayers Revolt.[19] The sixth member was also ambitious.[20] The majority of the entirely male committee were more interested in fiscal and political than educational issues, including the mayor, who sits as chairman.*

Melrose is also a conservative community, but with a long tradition. It has always been a "dry" district and has consistently refused to support a debt.[21] Until recently it was relatively quiet politically, with a low proportion of registered voters, as Table 3-4 indicated. It habitually voted Republican in gubernatorial and Presidential elections, as well as in local politics. In the elections of 1971, the first year for a full-time, salaried mayor, the first Italian Catholic was returned to office. At the same time, some of the citizens were becoming impatient about local spending and formed themselves into the "Thinking and Concerned Citizens for Low Taxes" (TAC). The TAC has waged some successful campaigns, with allies on the Board of Aldermen, including to help delay the building of a replacement high school. Yet in the five years

*This point was argued in a discussion with the Quincy superintendent over a previous draft. He claimed that the mayor said he was a politician, not an educator who thought "politician" was an honorable term. My statement that some school committee members were not "serving" out of civic duty was "scandalously inaccurate." In order to avoid more confusion, I understand these terms politician and civic duty to be categories of analysis with no pejorative meaning. They are used to distinguish types and substance of attitude to public roles.

Table 3-4. Registered Voters, 1970

Proportion of Total	Quincy	Melrose	Wellesley	Weston
Democrat	47.7	22.4	21.4	15.9
Republican	23.2	37.7	47.3	48.9

Source: U.S. population census.

to 1973 school enrollments have been such that high school pupils have had to operate on a double-session day.

The new fiscal concern, however, has not fully permeated the nine-member school committee. Eight of the members held office because their children were in public school and they regarded it as a civic duty. Political affiliation was not seen as important.[22] The ninth was a retired school administrator. The eight men were all in higher professional occupations and most were not politically ambitious. The one woman was a full-time housewife. Two young members, both lawyers and the newest members to the committee, were interested in other political offices but only in the long term. They were elected, as was one other member, on slates concerning the need for more "fiscal responsibility". The rest were elected because of their interest in a new high school. In fact, citizen interest in school elections was not very high. In 1971 there were only seven candidates for five posts, and the largest vote cast was only 7,000.[23]

Wellesley, like Quincy, is politically active, but for different reasons. Its citizens are concerned with their own local welfare, with strong interest in policies such as zoning and spending on amenities. The posts of town meeting moderator and selectmen are highly prized and influential political offices, and campaigns are vigorously waged, albeit only between shades of conservative opinion and between the long-standing citizens. Almost 50 percent of the citizens are registered Republican voters, as shown in Table 3-4, and the area invariably votes Republican in gubernatorial and Presidential elections. Indeed, the predominant concern locally is with fiscal efficiency. The advisory committee to the Town Meeting over financial matters is appointed by the Moderator. All its members are fiscally conservative businessmen who play a cautious role in monitoring expenditure.

School committee membership is seen as separate from other political posts. The five members in 1972 were on the committee because they had children in the schools and felt that they should hold some civic office.[24] They did not have greater ambitions. Nevertheless, there were strong differences of opinion about how to run the schools. The three men and one woman—a part-time teacher and housewife—had all been elected because of their interest in school spending. In fact, only two of them continued to pursue this aim. The fifth member, a housewife, was called the most liberal, a term she resented, because she was interested only in "sound educational practice" and not its cost. Interest in school elections in Wellesley is high. For example, there were six candidates for the two vacant posts in 1973.[25]

Weston is not obviously a politically conservative community, although in 1970 it had the highest proportion of registered Republican voters, as Table 3-4 clearly shows. It is, in fact, not very lively over local politics. The posts of moderator and selectmen are not highly contested; they have little responsibility since the school budget is two-thirds of the total.[26] For the 1973 elections, there were no eager candidates for a vacant selectman seat, so the chairman of the finance subcommittee had to be persuaded to stand.

The community, however, does have a strong and clear set of values. It is concerned with fiscal efficiency, which the appointed members of the finance committee actively work to ensure. The citizens are, at the same time, concerned to preserve their "lighthouse school system."[27] Indeed, a majority of citizens had children in the schools since they moved into the district in the first place because of the quality school system. The community supports only a small proportion of persons over 65: 6.7 percent compared with the Boston area average of 10.97 percent in 1965. Table 3-5 compares the districts. Clearly, it is predominantly a young community.

Yet school committee membership is not heavily sought. In the 1973 elections there were only three candidates for two seats, one of which was contested by its incumbent. As is customary, he was returned to office. Only one of the five members was elected because of his concern for finance,[28] even though he did not pursue this interest singlemindedly. Two members were professional educators, which was an unusual occurrence. One was a college administrator, considered an asset; the other, a single woman and counselor in a neighboring school system. The chairman in 1972 was originally persuaded to run for office by his predecessors because of his occupation as a labor-relations lawyer in a large company. He would be able to conduct salary negotiations with the teachers. The fifth member, a housewife, was elected because of her previous involvement in the townwide PTA.

Of the four districts, the citizens of Weston are apparently the most interested in the school system. Three points about this are worthy of mention. One is that they aimed to pay the highest teacher salaries in the state and by 1972 were rivalled only by Boston.[29] For a long time, Wellesley was a close competitor. Secondly, their school buildings have all been renewed in the last decade and provide a host of facilities including swimming pools and

Table 3-5.   Age Distribution of Populations, 1965

	Quincy	*Melrose*	*Wellesley*	*Weston*
Proportion Aged over 65 of Total Population	12.3	11.9	10.0	6.7

Source: State census.

athletic tracks. Many parents are involved in the townwide PTA which is a social and fund-raising organization for extra-school amenities. Thirdly, the town boasts a very low pupil-teacher ratio. The teachers are not well organized. They do have a professional association which is affiliated to the Massachusetts Teachers Association (MTA), but it is of recent origin. The school-based administrators reluctantly were members. Indeed, collective bargaining and formal contracts began only in 1971. Previously a memorandum of agreement was formulated annually.[30]

Weston differs from the other areas in its wealth and related age structure. It has few controversies over educational spending. In Wellesley, which is almost as wealthy, a larger proportion of the population are older [32] : 10 percent in 1965 were over 65 as shown in Table 3-5. They, obviously, were not very interested in the school system. They compete with parents over priorities for local spending. Nevertheless, Wellesley boasts high teacher salary scales (for a comparison, see Table 3-6) and a basically adequate stock of school buildings. However, in 1972 the high school was in need of extension, given growing pupil enrollments, and the neighborhood policy for elementary schools needed revision. The town had an average pupil-teacher ratio and also pursued a generous policy of educational aides and voluntary parental involvement in the elementary schools. The parents are also well organized into PTA's, particularly at the elementary schools. The teachers recently became organized into a professional association, actively pursuing more militant policies, especially over salary and working conditions. For the 1972-3 contract they even threatened strike action and demonstrated against the school committee. Negotiations were finally settled by state arbitration.[32]

Melrose, being less wealthy, is less able to provide generous teachers' salary scales—they are about the state average—or buildings. Its committee also has to compete against those citizens who are not interested in the school system. In 1965, for example, 11.9 percent were over 65 years old. Its high school was in dire need of extension. This need was finally being met, albeit five years after it was perceived and advocated. Some of its elementary schools were old, but only one had received aid through Title I of the Elementary and Secondary Education Act (ESEA).[33] The parents do not actively demand change, although each school has a PTA. Yet in the last five years the pupil-teacher ratio has improved from 30:1 to 22:1. The teachers are no longer quiescent. They organized into the Melrose Educational Association, which became militant in

Table 3-6. Teacher Salary Scales, March 1971

	Quincy	Melrose	Wellesley	Weston
Maximum	$12,150	$13,503	$13,725	$14,800
Minimum	$ 7,500	$ 7,500	$ 7,700	$ 7,850

Source: Massachusetts Teachers Association, Research Bulletin No. 712-9.

its collective bargaining. For the 1972-3 contract, negotiations lasted through the summer vacation and strike action was proposed.[34] This was a repeat of the previous year's events.

Quincy, however, is the most volatile in educational matters, partly because of its age structure and also its lack of wealth. It had 12.3 percent of its population over 65 in 1965. Moreover, in 1970 over 20 percent of the school population attended the local parochial schools compared to the others (see Table 3-7). In the fall of 1972 unemployment was running at 7 to 8 percent. Its school buildings were not modern. Two high schools were recently extended; a new vocational technical high school was built in 1965, and some of the 21 elementary and 2 junior high schools were slowly renewed during the last two decades.[35] Six of the elementary schools received funds under Title I of ESEA. The pupil-teacher ratio was considered quite high—19:1 in 1972—partly because of the lack of teaching space.[36] Teachers' salaries, like those of Melrose, are around the Boston average. In recent years the Quincy Educational Association has therefore adopted a more militant strategy for collective bargaining. For the 1972-3 contract, for example, the teachers took a day off and demonstrated in protest against conditions.[37] Contracts were not settled until the second week of the academic year.

Although the administrators of the school systems were similar in their educational training, they also contrasted with one another and bore some resemblance to their respective communities. Quincy's school superintendent was born and raised in the area. He is of Irish Catholic and Canadian descent.[38] He began his career as a local teacher and rapidly worked his way through the system to become superintendent at the age of 35. Several of his colleagues, nine administrators who compose the Learning Management Team, were local products. The main interest of the Quincy superintendent was in educational policy, and he has successfully pioneered kindergartens, special education, guidance, and community colleges as well as improving on vocational education. Quincy established the first junior college in the state. His chief policy was the Student Centered Learning System, to facilitate individual rather than group learning.

Melrose's superintendent was equally interested in developing educational policy. His aim was also individualisation. He has already implemented it since coming to the district in 1968. As an Irish Catholic, he did not grow up

Table 3-7. School-Attending Children, 1970

	Quincy	*Melrose*	*Wellesley*	*Weston*
Public Schools	16,735	7,556	5,902	2,853
Non-Public Schools	3,022	729	1,104	407
Total	19,757	8,285	7,006	3,260
Proportion in Public	80%	89%	84%	87%

Source: Mass. Department of Commerce and Development.

in Melrose, but in a neighboring district of Boston. He had few allegiances to
the area but rather was committed to a career as a professional educator. His
two chief colleagues, however, were local products and likely to remain loyal to
the district.[39]

Wellesley's superintendent originates from New Hampshire and
began his career in educational research and management. He was less interested in educational policy than in its effective management through business
techniques.[40] He himself refused a contract for his job but would work until
there were an irreconcilable conflict. His two assistants were also cosmopolitan
in their orientation. One worked in industry until becoming Wellesley's business
manager; the other was a professor of education.

Weston's superintendent was appointed from New York State. He
was more interested in the smooth running of the system than in its development.
The same is true for his business assistant, formerly assistant high school
principal, and his assistant for personnel. The two coordinators managed
educational policy.[41]

BUDGET HISTORY

Each community has developed different budgetary traditions both in attitudes
to spending and actual practices. Strategies have been developed because of
national inflation and new business practices. All four communities have tried
to reduce overall spending but only in proportion to former rates of increase.
Wellesley and Weston have continued to spend either absolutely or relatively
more than Quincy and Melrose, as Table 3-8 shows. In the 1960s, the rates of
increase in Quincy and Melrose were about 10 percent per annum, whereas in
Weston and Wellesley they were over 14 percent.

Cuts in educational spending have depended upon citizens' concerns
and problems. As Barber pointed out:

> Most boards appear to recognize that cutting budget requests 'across
> the board' by some fixed percentage or amount is in the long run,
> destructive of budgetary rationality.[42]

Each emphasised some component, perhaps to the detriment of the rest of the
system. Weston's school committee chose to pay its teachers well and squeeze
on consumable and fixed supplies. Wellesley continued to refine its school
support services, such as the curriculum center. It did not maintain its position
at the top of the league in teachers' salaries. Melrose retained its strong interest
in extramural activities. Quincy put its emphasis on vocational education and
teaching methods.

Prior to the 1970s, all four used a traditional budgetary method,
seeing the system as a family business. By convention they left the content and

Table 3-8.   Budget Expenditures for Year Ending 30 June, 1971

	Instruction	*Total*
Quincy	$13,239,938	$16,741,377
Melrose	$ 5,098,427	$ 6,319,893
Wellesley	$ 5,924,499	$ 7,649,584
Weston	$ 2,842,517	$ 3,967,766

Source: Mass. Department of Education: annual statistics.

allocation of resources in the budget to the school administrators.[43]   Each committee saw the budget as a narrow area of decision-making. It was not susceptible to representative or citizen influence. The members disdained detailed comment. They did not press for business techniques. However, they did see spending as a sensitive, political issue. Committee deliberations were held in private, prior to public announcement. Their discussions were indirect and centered on educational policies or developments.

One year in Quincy, for example, the chairman asked the superintendent, immediately on receipt of the proposed budget, if he had everything he needed. When the superintendent replied in the affirmative, the chairman moved budget approval. The superintendent, surprised, insisted that the committee at least inspect it. The chairman's response was to concur and defer the decision until the next meeting. Nevertheless, he did not take his budget book home. At the next meeting he took out the book he had left in the committee rooms. Without opening it, he moved its approval. The motion was seconded and passed without any budget review.

The situation has now changed in all four communities, partly because some members have an interest in low educational spending. More businesslike procedures to simplify budget evaluation have been adopted as a result of changing practices in local and federal government.[44] The budget has become a mechanism for evaluating school policies rather then being merely a continuing contract with personnel. But practice varies.

Quincy, both because of its new superintendent and more apparent large-scale organization, has developed detailed categories of expenditure in the context of a line-item budget. It follows the procedures the state enjoins and has improved only its accounting methods.[45] This has involved administrators in more rigorous budgetary preparation and definitions of intentions.[46]

The Melrose administrators became interested in new business practices as a result of external stimulation. Other local professional educators were pursuing new accounting methods. Progress was slow because the business management frequently changed hands. Program budgeting was only started in 1972. The cycle under study involves the second year of implementation. The method used is still only a modification of the traditional line-item budget: to have comparative data on expense, first instructional and later technical items. Developments have been piecemeal because there was no external consultation.

Wellesley's thrust towards better business practice has been the greatest. It came from both the schoolmen and the political representatives. Indeed, the school committee, having deliberately chosen a superintendent interested in business administration, demanded a complete overhaul of the budgetary process. First, the superintendent was helped by two business professors. He started to develop a program budget. As a result, all the town departments became interested. For the 1973-4 budget the whole municipality hired the services of a firm of accountants and consultants to help it with program budgeting. The eventual aim was to develop a whole system of PPB—planning, programming and budgeting. This process involved a new approach in 1972 to budget consideration to include program and policy evaluation rather than an annual scrutiny of individual items. It also changed the responsibilities of participants in the school system.

Weston's administrators had also developed an interest in budgetary methods. They have not moved as quickly or effectively as in Wellesley. Members of the task force, set up three years before and consisting of elected members, an interested citizen, and administrators, felt that a cautious strategy was necessary.[47] Immediate implementation of program budgeting would reveal costs, such as those for athletics, with implications which the school committee could not present to the public. In 1972 the administrators applied a program budget format in three areas: over transportation, pupil services, and foreign languages overall resources. For 1973-4 the administrators effected a complete program budget alone. They developed a rudimentary set of expenditure categories for all programs.

These changes have affected the perceptions of committee members of their role. Twenty-one of the twenty-six members interviewed considered budgeting to be one of their most important tasks. Its definition is conditioned by their motives as public officials. Those members interested in "fiscal responsibility" see their main obligation as that of "paring down the budget" and ensuring reasonable spending. Those who serve out of interest in education have a wider concept of budgeting and its role in educational policy. They see it as a mechanism to evaluate the policies and direction of the system. Some thought that the budget paring had gone too far and their task now was to ensure that "the system was not hurting in the educational programs."[48] Only five members considered educational policy per se more important than budgeting. They admit that the budget is a vital consideration.[49] The members have difficulty in specifying their crucial tasks, because, as one member said: "Budgeting and the determination of educational programs are a seamless web."[50]

Budgeting, which once was treated as an administrative matter, has become a major task of school committees and, therefore, school administrators. Only one other task is regarded as equally important. The members interviewed all stated that the hiring of a competent superintendent was crucial. He should understand and work with the values of the community. If the community acquires a good superintendent, it can entrust him with the task of running the system without constant recourse to the committee. The two essential issues are budgeting and work with professional educators.

However, the actual importance of the superintendent to the members may vary with the task. He may only be the key figure in the school system for purely educational matteɪs requiring expertise or administrative or technical knowledge. Financial decisions may not need such expertise. The superintendent may not be used as decision formulator but only as an advisor for the budget. The citizens and their representatives may play a definite role in the determination of expenditures, both the total and the substance. It is to this specific interaction between the community and its professional educators that I now turn.

SUMMARY

I have portrayed the four communities and shown their variation in political structure, attitudes and conventional practices over budgeting. I now start with an analysis of the operating budget formulation by the professional educators in the context of the community.

NOTES TO CHAPTER THREE

1. From *City and Town Monograph for Quincy,* printed by the Mass. Department of Commerce and Development, revised March 1972.
2. *Ibid.*
3. Data from *City and Town Monograph for Melrose,* printed by the Mass. Department of Commerce and Development, revised March 1972.
4. Data from *City and Town Monograph for Wellesley,* printed by the Mass. Department of Commerce and Development, revised March 1972.
5. Data from *City and Town Monograph for Weston,* printed by the Mass. Department of Commerce and Development, revised March 1972.
6. *Op. cit., Quincy City and Town Monograph.* The superintendent also produced figures in the Annual Report of Quincy schools 1972, *viz:*

Year	School Enrollment
1969	16,588
1970	16,949
1972	16,488

7. *Wellesley City and Town Monograph, op. cit.*
8. David and Holly Franke, *Safe Places of the USA* (New York: Arlington, 1972). See also an unpublished paper by Dorothy Ulig, *Together and Alone in Suburbia* (Harvard Graduate School of Education, 1972).
9. E.H. Goss, *History of Melrose* (Mass.: City of Melrose, 1902), p. 58.
10. *op. cit., Weston City and Town Monograph.*
11. Data from US census of 1960; *Weston City and Town Monograph, op. cit.* For comparisons with the four districts, see Table 3–1.

12. *Ibid;* see Table 3–2.
13. *Ibid;* see Table 3–3.
14. *Weston City and Town Monograph, op. cit.*
15. *Wellesley City and Town Monograph, op. cit.*
16. *Melrose City and Town Monograph, op. cit.*
17. For registered voter patterns, see Table 3–4. Information from interview with Walter Hannon, January 18, 1973.
18. Interviews with Daniel Raymondi and Harold Davis on January 18, 1973, in Quincy, Mass.
19. Interviews with Charles Sweeny, January 19, 1973, and Francis Anselmo, January 18, 1973.
20. Interview with Paul Kelly, January 25, 1973.
21. In 1970 the debt was only 0.9% of equalized valuation. Data from Massachusetts Teachers Association, Research Bulletin No. 712-9, March 1971.
22. From interviews with Dr. Chuck Crocetti, Dr. Robert Soule, Paul Butler, Richard Pierce, David Guthrow, Ernest Murphy, Bud Pendleton, John Coughlan—eight of the nine committee members, held in January 1973.
23. Data from the city clerk.
24. From interviews with Jean Kelly, Ruth Walter, Robert Harvey, Horace Schermerhorn, and David McNeish, January-February 1973, in Wellesley.
25. Data from the town's clerk.
26. In 1971 the school tax rate was $22, and the general rate $34. See Weston's *City and Town Monograph, op. cit.*
27. This phrase was used frequently to me by Drs. Wood and Stayn in interviews, January-February 1973, in Weston, Mass.
28. From interviews with Mary Horne, Joan Wexler, Peter Richardson, Charles Sutherland, and Ted Phillips, January-February 1973.
29. Statement at the Public Hearing, March 10, 1973, by Ted Phillips.
30. Interview with Ted Phillips, *op. cit.*
31. See Table 2–3. But Assessed Valuations per capita in 1971 were Weston $16,843; Wellesley, $9,618.
32. Interviews with Mrs. Jean Kelly and Mr. Claridge, February 1973.
33. Information from the superintendent, Melrose 1973.
34. Interview with Don Mack, January 16, 1973.
35. Discussion with Dr. Creedon, July 1973.
36. *Ibid.*
37. Interview with Harold Crowley. *The Patriot Ledger*—a local newspaper— reports for October 1973.
38. Discussion with Dr. Creedon, *op. cit.*
39. Interviews with Drs. Quin and Bachelder, and Mr. Driscoll, December 1972.
40. Interviews with Drs. Goodman and Muto and Mr. Lyndon, January 1973.
41. Interviews with Drs. Wood, Stayn, MacDonald, and Kennedy, January 1973.
42. James D. Barber, *Power in Committees* (Chicago: Rand McNally, 1966), p. 38.
43. Interviews with Mr. W. Phinney and Mr. F. Nolan, January 6, 1973.

44. Barber, *op. cit.*
45. Interviews with Steven Moynihan, January 6, 1973.
46. *Ibid.*
47. Interview with Mr. John Stayn, January 1973.
48. Interviews with David McNeish and Dick Pierce, *op. cit.*
49. Not one dismissed although a number saw it as a chore.
50. Interview with Ernest Murphy, January 3, 1973.

Chapter Four

Preparing Budget Proposals

In this chapter I shall discuss preparations for the 1973-4 budget, extending over an 18-month period. First, the existing machinery and use made of it by participants is described. A summary of the initial decisions taken is presented. The initiators of the proposals are seen as the professional educators, whose methods are, however, heavily influenced by their community's characteristics. Professionalism in budgeting is therefore explained by the constraints that these impose upon the professional educators as well as by the nature of the task.

Preparation here refers only to the operating budget; it does not include preparation for the salary negotiations either with professional or nonprofessional personnel. Because of the peculiar nature of the budgetary cycle in Massachusetts, the two aspects have traditionally been seen as separate but integral parts of budgeting. Until the year under study, the operating budget was prepared for a calendar year. Salaries for the majority of personnel, that is, teachers and administrators, were settled for the academic year. Thus each school budget would include two salary contracts—one in use for the existing year and one for the following year. Given these time differences, the two issues have proceeded in parallel. I shall therefore look first at the operating budget.

The operating budget can be viewed independently of the administration of the school system. The key professional educators define it as a self-contained activity and deal with it separately from other areas of policy-making. This separation may be artificial. Although the educational system is broken down into a series of annual events, these are arbitrary divisions superimposed upon a continuous process. In that respect, the budget develops from issues of previous years. Decisions taken in any one are the consequences of past policies. In any one year few changes may be sought. The system may be working to the satisfaction of most citizens, or those who are dissatisfied may have no means of expressing their wishes that things be altered. In any one year it may not even be possible to effect all the changes thought necessary. It may happen, too, that changes are made which may arise from policy decisions other than those in the budget. But, since this process is ostensibly distinct from other policy-making and contains a clear set of machinery, I shall confine my discussion to it. Non-decisions, that is, decisions taken negatively and that produce changes only over a long time span, may therefore be missed in an analysis of the overt steps.[1] However, the focus, which is upon the regular interactions of the participants in the education system, will be apparent in this review.

THE GENERAL MACHINERY

In Massachusetts the cycle used to start in the spring preceding the year for which the budget was prepared. It started immediately after the budget for the current year had been ratified. Until 1973 budgets were finalized for the calendar year by April 1st of that year. For example, the Melrose Ordinances stated:

> The Board of Aldermen shall appropriate annually before the first day of April the amount necessary to meet the expenditure of the city for the current financial year.[2]

In general, the professional educators begin by stating their requests. The municipal and school representatives may play a role in setting guidelines or a budget ceiling. Because the school committees officially have fiscal autonomy, directives from municipal officials may ostensibly be ignored. The school committees may hold meetings to initiate the new preparations. Pressure groups may also be involved either formally or informally and as lay citizens, parents, or pupils. There is no official state machinery, although the state ruled in 1972 that student participation in decisions should be increased.[3]

MACHINERY IN THE FOUR COMMUNITIES

The school committees do not make the first move by gathering views of lay citizens or parents and pupils. Municipal officials may make statements to guide the process, but they do not start it. The role of the community and its representatives is entirely informal. Although there were no special public meetings on budget preparation in 1972, all four school committees hold regular, open meetings at which citizens could present their requests or budgetary needs, thus providing a basis for the professional educators' work. The two towns, Wellesley and Weston, have open forums at the beginning of their regular meetings to encourage public input. Wellesley call this its "Citizen Speak" session.[4] Weston just implemented such sessions, *viz:*

In 1971 the committee continued its policy adopted last year of
designating the first half hour of the first meeting of each month
as an open forum thus encouraging community members to bring
questions and concerns to the school committee and school
administration.[5]

Moreover, in all four districts there are parent organizations which
could be consulted over budget changes. However, PTA's are commonly regarded
as support for individual school systems.[6] The incidence of PTA's varies. In
Quincy not every school has a PTA, and those that exist are as a result of the
principal's rather then the parents' initiative. In Melrose the PTA's do not see
themselves as initiators but receivers of policy from the administrators. In
Wellesley all the schools have PTA's to provide support for school policies. In
Weston the one townwide parent organization is not involved in budget preparation, although its concerns are to provide *additional* school funds.

The PTA's may be used more informally, either by individual
members, professional educators, or by school principals. However, this method
of communication was cited only by one respondent.[7] Preparing the budget
does not formally include parents.

Recently pupils have been recognized as a formal group. Student
councils were formed in high schools in the four districts. They were asked to
submit their recommendations, with or without financial implications, to the
school committees. In two districts—Quincy and Wellesley—student representatives regularly attended and contributed to school committee meetings. Furthermore, the Quincy superintendent exhorted the principals and teachers to involve
students in the budget proposals.[8] In Melrose and Weston, mechanisms for
involving students were not so routine. Special meetings were held between
students and school committees, separate from regular meetings.

Thus the citizens are not completely excluded from the preparations.
Machinery exists for parental and student participation or input. The administrators need not start their work without knowledge of the key consumers. Moreover, they have some information about general citizen preferences.

SOURCES OF COMMUNITY ATTITUDES

Community values are usually expressed through elections. Some recent
members on all the school committees had been elected on slates about "fiscal
responsibility".[9] In Quincy four of seven members, new in January 1971,
had used spending rather than educational advance as their platform.[10]
In Melrose, too, the three most recent of the nine member committee stressed
concern about the tax rate. In Wellesley four of the five members had been
elected on a "frugal" slate. Weston alone had only a minority chiefly concerned
with spending, rather than education. The overwhelming view of newer members

in the four districts was that the community should take a more responsible attitude towards spending. This contrasted with that of older members who were, on the whole, more interested in providing a "quality educational system."

Given this situation, there was no real need for financial guidelines to circumscribe the budget activities. Nevertheless, the committees were not completely autonomous; they had to obtain revenue to finance their projected spending from the municipal officials. They could not be entirely oblivious to their opinions. Moreover, recently state officials were suggesting abolishing fiscal autonomy in a further attempt to curb "reckless spending." A decision by the Supreme Court of Massachusetts in 1972 was a cause of real concern in the cities. The mayor of Malden's decision to cut the school committee budget was upheld. The budget had not been submitted by the statutory deadline. Also a bill was presented in late 1972 to the State Legislature to abolish fiscal autonomy in the towns.

Financial attitudes had been articulated by some, if not the majority, of citizens in the municipalities. In three communities, as noted in Chapter 3, special groups had been set up to monitor local government spending. They constantly pressed for a reduction in the annual rate of increase of taxes. In Quincy and Melrose there were independent pressure groups as well as the municipal officials urging frugality. In Wellesley and Weston the finance committees alone urged thriftiness. The superintendent in Weston found this a particularly difficult circumstance:

> The superintendent's dilemma here in Weston is that the finance committee are always pleading for reduced spending and yet citizens come to live here especially for the schools.[12]

A more stark instance of this financial concern is important for the school budget. It concerns new school building. Although school buildings are not finally decided by school committees, community attitudes toward the necessity for renewal affect other decisions. Buildings are decided and financed locally. During the 1960s school enrollments in the four school districts continued the national trend of the 1950s and increased at a steady rate. New buildings were required in all four to accommodate the larger school population.

Weston was unique in that its new buildings had been completed by the end of the last decade. There was no real acrimony between citizens. In Quincy, building need had not yet been exhausted. School supporters had experienced difficulty getting financial sanction for high school additions. In 1972 the city council were reluctant to sanction bond issues for a new sports complex and administration building. During budget deliberations early in 1973, architectural specifications which had already been commissioned were rejected. The city council saw them as too costly and unnecessary.[13] Melrose had developed at least three separate plans for high or junior high school extensions. The community was loathe to agree to a bond issue. By late 1972 it had gone so far as to sanction architectural specifications after two referenda. Wellesley's high school did not meet state standards. Yet a high school addition was a controversy in 1972. In the September architectural specifications were voted on. It was not certain that the town meeting of 1973 would approve the necessary bond issue of $5.6 million. All the communities were becoming deeply conscious of the need to "curb public spending and fight inflation."

SCHOOL COMMITTEE GUIDELINES

Because of the economic situation in 1972, the superintendents formulated budget guidelines early in the year, to which they asked their committees to agree. Melrose's guidelines informally agreed in the late spring of 1972 were that there should be no new programs or personnel and that they should hold back on new equipment in anticipation of a new high school, scheduled for opening in 1974-5. Wellesley's guidelines were formulated and discussed at two meetings in the summer of 1972, to enable early moves to program budgeting. The town meeting in March 1972 had voted a sum for consultant fees. The guidelines were that there should only be a 5 percent increase in nonpersonnel costs to cover inflation and:

> that the total budget will be no greater than the amount required
> to pay for enrollment increases (only at senior high school) inflation,
> negotiation increases and state mandated programs.[15]

In Weston, the school committee had informally adopted a set of guidelines for the 1972 budget which should hold. They were that the pupil-teacher ratio should be checked for programs where it was liable to be low—specifically, foreign languages. No other program or personnel changes were mooted.

MUNICIPAL GUIDELINES

The municipal officials did not issue early clear guidelines. In the two cities the mayor was ultimately responsible for the tax rate. In Quincy the new mayor put forward his stance in his acceptance speech in no uncertain terms:

> I intend to conduct an economy minded administration because
> the houseowner and rentpayer are hurting in the pocketbook and
> deserve an end to spiralling costs.[15]

In his capacity as mayor he was chairman of the school committee. He would help develop the budget. He did issue guidelines for his own departments which enjoined no new personnel or programs.[16] The school administrators had a yardstick by which to judge their proposals.

In Melrose the new mayor was said only to be conscious of the "tide of the times." He did not issue guidelines until the fall of 1972. They were for *all* his departments, calling for *no* increase in the non-salary spending of 1973 over 1972. He was unable to put such a tight control on salary spending, he announced publicly at a school committee meeting.[17] By then the committee and its administrators had already advanced their budget preparation. The committee, determined to retain its autonomy, refused to endorse the guidelines. They did counsel the superintendent to take note.

In the two towns, the town meeting members were ultimately responsible for the tax rate. Their appointed finance committee would monitor spending. In Weston no new guidelines were issued for 1973-4, although the finance committee did voice its concern. At the Wellesley town meeting in 1970, they specified a maximum 8 percent annual budget increase.[18] Nevertheless, the advisory committee issued, in the fall of 1972, more stringent guidelines, a result of changed economic circumstances. The school administrators had already progressed a long way, with more generous guidelines, and felt justified to continue.

SCHOOL COMMITTEE CONTRIBUTIONS

The school committees did not get much more involved in budget preparation than just ratifying guidelines. They did not initiate discussion on finance or further the impact of policies on the budget. But the administrators were not operating entirely in a vacuum. Policies which form core needs are continuous and are constantly scrutinized by school committees, if not for their financial implications. No routine or statutory timetable exists; they are handled as issued. No policies were discussed explicitly in relation to budget formulation. This may have been because the members were satisfied with existing programs or because they lacked knowledge of the effect on the budget. It may also have been because the budget had been defined as a matter separate from other policy.

The elected members did involve themselves in two issues. One, a direct outcome of financial concern, was the need to improve business practices. Only in Wellesley did the committee become deeply involved. The committee employed consultants, first academics and second accountants, to improve budget formulation. As a result, the committee members were taught the procedures of program budgeting. In the other districts ،ne administrators themselves improved the system's management. They got committee approval but did not spell out their actual practices to them.

The other issue was devising an 18-month rather than a 12-month budget. This would have both technical or administrative complications and political impact. Most important would be the apparent increase in the tax rate. The committees had both to consider how to administer and present it to the public. The state administrators had not set out criteria, for they only: " . . .

aid process of setting policy with interpretation of the pertinent acts."[19]
The committees asked their superintendents to present proposals. The local
community, elected and lay citizens, did not contribute much to the preparations. Indeed, their involvement was not really solicited. Their views merely
provided the backcloth to the administrators' work. This confirms James'
finding about the incorporation of public officials into the process—they are
there only at the behest of the administrators.[20]

THE PROFESSIONAL EDUCATORS' PROCEDURES

Ostensible preparation was initiated by the professional educators. Methods
varied both because of community needs and superintendent preferences.
First the budgets were formulated by the superintendents in collaboration
with the other professional educators. But who was involved depended upon
the superintendent's assessment of his role and importance. Notions of system
management affected whether the superintendent asked all or a selection of
teachers to contribute ideas. Teacher involvement was also mediated by administrative structure. Size of community affected administrative numbers, as did
wealth. On a per pupil basis, as Table 4-1 shows, Weston had more senior
administrators and coordinators than Quincy, Melrose, or Wellesley. Size and
wealth are not the only factors affecting administrative style. A crucial factor
is the superintendent's professional image. This is, however, rooted in the local
political culture. All the superintendents view themselves as educators but
modify their practical strategies to suit local conditions. This is inevitable
because committees select superintendents to fit their needs. The Quincy and
Melrose superintendents were the most determined educators; Wellesley's
superintendent was as interested in management as in education per se, and
Weston's superintendent was equivocal. They pursued a conciliatory administrative style with their committee and colleagues.[21] These professional styles
affect which of the professional educators were involved in the budget.

Table 4-1. **Professional Employees in the Four School Districts for
Year Ending June, 1971**

	Quincy	*Melrose*	*Wellesley*	*Weston*
Administrators	175	24	24	12
Teachers	855	382	345	165
Teacher Aides	25	6	DR	19
Supervisors	10	47	17	DR
Total	1,064	459	386	196
Number of Public School Children	16,735	7,556	5,902	2,853
Ratio of Pupils to Professionals	15:1	16:1	15:1	14:1

Source: Mass. Department of Education statistics.

Teachers and principals first formulated tentative budgets within superintendent financial or policy guidelines. This was done on a school-by-school basis. Teacher organizations were not initially involved. Needs were viewed in a school, rather than teaching, context. Responsibilities varied among the teachers and administrators.

In Quincy the superintendent's creed was: "He who is to be affected by a decision ought to be involved in the process of making that decision." [22] He relied on delegaton of duties and individual administrative responsibility. His administrative organization had grown over his five years as superintendent; from 10 to 16 central office administrators, coordinators or directors for every educational program, in addition to departmental heads at the high schools. They were asked to collaborate with principals and departmental heads or teachers. Each principal had to plan a school budget with staff, students and parents, focusing on such concerns as learning materials, equipment, plant and personnel needs. Each had to state goals for five years to fit with the superintendent's goals. The requests were assessed in "program analysis grids" by the Instructional Planning Team (IPT)—the directors and three senior administrators for instruction. The priorities were evaluated and resources allocated for three separate categories: capital outlay, and general and instructional supplies. The principals, acting as a district team, determined the priorities for plant and renovations. Administrators evaluated personnel needs and plant operation.

The Melrose superintendent had a more autocratic attitude toward budget building. He wanted to fit requests to his policies. Plant needs were assessed by one technical administrator. Principals at the elementary schools and directors or coordinators at high schools submitted composite requests for supplies, equipment and personnel. High school principals had few direct responsibilities.

In Wellesley each principal had school responsibility and submitted requests for all resources. These were on the basis of submissions from program leaders on needs and changes, given explicit program goals. The superintendent had originally provided sample goals and added: "It is important that each program's goals be well thought out. In other words, the goals should identify the changes that are expected in the persons and programs they serve." [23] Coordinators were not involved in budget building. The emphasis there was on individual program responsibility. The superintendent coordinated the process but did not press for a policy.

In Weston, the process was very lengthy and detailed for the first time. Each program leader arrived at his request for all resources with his subordinate teachers. He submitted a statement with a policy review first to his principal and second to a committee of program directors and principals. Plant needs were reviewed separately. The two-stage scrutiny dealt with instructional programs in order to enable more concise educational appraisal.

Parents and pupils may have made actual contributions here.

Quincy's flow chart later presented to the committee spelled this out.[24] Only one respondent, in Melrose, mentioned any pressure or input. There, one elementary PTA vigorously argued for more school supplies, organizing a party to persuade the superintendent. Parents and pupils were not positively involved. The superintendent in Melrose stressed that they were deliberately excluded. He and the committee defined the process as too technical to allow for direct public contributions. The preparatory process is strictly bureaucratic or administrative.

ADMINISTRATIVE OVERVIEW

The superintendent and the central office administrators reviewed the budget requests of the program leaders. They assessed priorities. This review varied because of, first, administrative organization and, second, perceived needs. In Quincy and Weston a wide range of administrators were involved in decision-making. In Wellesley and Melrose reviews were by fewer administrators and the most senior ones at that. This is partly due to size of staff related either to size of community or its welath. The differences were not crucial to the outcomes of budget proposals, though they did affect internal relations in the educational profession.

In Quincy the budget review was undertaken by the Learning Management Team (LMT)—nine senior administrators chaired and directed by the superintendent. All decisions were taken by the whole team, with formal motions proposed and voted on. The most time was spent on supplies rather than plant or personnel, taking a full 10 days. A dress rehearsal by the IPT and LMT was held to ensure the budget recommendations' adequacy for the school committee.[25] No teachers or principals were involved.

In Melrose the review was shorter and less elaborate. The superintendent did not extol the virtues of personal responsibility. He dealt with all the budget requests to establish an efficient and effective school system. The requests were reviewed by a team of the superintendent, his associate for instruction, and business assistant. It took about a week. The key issues were supplies and equipment. Individual hearings were then held for the program leaders to defend requests. As the result of a strong plea, some reversals were made to the final proposals.

In Wellesley the superintendent put emphasis on individual accountability. He analyzed requests with consultants. The plant needs were assessed separately. The Staff Advisory Council, 12 representative teachers and principals, and Staff Executive Council, principals, coordinators and administrators, were to review the requests. Because of problems developing program goals, this stage was omitted, and the proposals were finalized by the senior administrators alone.

In Weston the process was more complex: for the first time two newly appointed program directors aided the superintendent and his business assistant to review requests. This was to review the general operation of policy. They not only inspected budget requests financially but interrogated program leaders about their programs. They wanted subjective rather than standard criteria of assessment. Four stages of review were eventually undertaken. The main thrust was program evaluation and stock-taking in order to get rid of the traditional poker game approach. The four stages covered policy and program analysis individually and collectively by schools. The process took longer than predicted because of the problem of changing the principals' expectations; they did not easily adapt to the new style of bargaining and evaluation.

Thus the administrator's tasks were differently defined in each school district. The differences related to the boundaries of decisions, and centered around educational policy, its complementary administrative and technical aspects. The professional tasks of the educators are not simple. This is more obvious by reference to the type and substance of reviews.

REVIEW METHODS

There was no systematic way to evaluate requests. Precedent and knowledge of the system was relied on. Few formulae were used to evaluate equitable needs or the distribution of resources. Revenue was not considered. The terms of reference were purely habitual expenditure. In Quincy, some resources had usually been allocated by formulae, such as supplies and learning materials, which were retained. Given the declining enrollment and yet inflation, the actual figure was revised per pupil.[26] The evaluation school by school was changed to an individual analysis over all resources, to have more knowledge of the system. But the analysis still relied on a comparison with previous years' estimated appropriations rather than actual spending.

In Melrose the approach was to consider programs, not personnel, using elementary schools as a whole and high school programs. No formulae were used, but comparison was made with actual rather than appropriated expenditure of the previous year: by proration. Equipment was most rigorously reviewed, given the likelihood of a new high school and its need for special equipment. Declining elementary enrollments for 1972-3 helped financial stringency. The review was very ad hoc, to consider programs with an intuitive view of their merits. Typical superintendent comments were:

> I've given him what he wanted and so there is no problem although his budget is up. He's a new principal and the old was thrifty. . . . The principal at Lincoln is careful and so I don't question. I gave him more than last year. . . .
> Cut the principal at Mann because he's got too much stuff. I just visited the school and made a mental note. . . .

> She tends to ask for the moon. . . .
> The two new media girls are unreal! They pumped out a budget to
> show us what the department should look like and to get what they
> want. . . .
> It's unreal—give them the same as last year and tell them to use
> their own judgment in substituting. . . .[24]

In Wellesley the emphasis was different again. An attempt was made
to consider each program on its own merits; by reference to stated long-term
goals. No comparison with the previous year's spending was made. Interest was
in reviewing suggested program changes requiring funds. Alternate ways to
achieve change had to be stated. The superintendent took the decisions on
program changes and their particular methods. He could only sanction a small
number because of his stringent guidelines. In Weston the review focused on
both comparison with the previous year and espoused adequacy of program.
No formulae were used to compare schools or programs. Each program was
inspected for its pupil-teacher ratio and relation to school organization.

The process of review was very lengthy in all four areas. It became
more explicit and deliberately evaluative.

BUDGET PRIORITIES

The actual changes made to the budgets differed on two counts. One was community needs and past priorities and the other was superintendent preferences,
in the light of potential committee reactions. Although the situation clearly
called for financial stringency, none of the budget proposals represented just
maintenance of the status quo or mere inflationary increases. Certainly no
budget contained a system cutback. Zero-base reviews were not conducted.
The administrators therefore had to probe their school systems to justify
changes they would make. The changes were made on an ad hoc basis and
through individual pressure.

All superintendents spent most of the time screening instructional
programs and their needs. Personnel needs were barely alluded to mainly because
of the strict local guidelines. It was only in Weston that they were considered.
The final review consisted of juggling staff ratios between schools and programs
to reduce high school foreign languages and elementary art and music. Few
teachers could be dismissed because of state tenure laws, yet superfluous teachers were not all equally flexible to reallocate. The actual changes were small and
not costly.

In Wellesley one program change thought necessary related to
personnel. The guidelines enjoined staff increases. The change was termed a
trade-off with a redundant coordinator post to make it palatable. The other
changes concerned instruction which was either essential, such as industrial

arts or elementary music, or peripheral, and later called "educational frills," such as a curriculum center, food services, research and development. The other superintendents ensured adequacy of the instructional programs through their supplies. In Quincy, for example, certain cushions were retained through expired programs that had been financed mainly with federal aid. They changed the name to the Student Centered Learning System program. This would not be presented to the committee as a change, but internally it would render system improvements.

The 18-month budget complicated the issue. Yet increases, which were felt to be educationally necessary or desirable but which might be opposed by committee, were easier to obscure. The problem was variously tackled: each used a particular method to avoid mention of a necessary large increase in spending. All based budgets on one year, either calendar or academic, and added on for the extra six months. Quincy considered its budget for the calendar year 1973. It prorated items for 1974, with various factors designed to indicate habitual spending patterns, particularly on supplies. Melrose converted to the new fiscal cycle immediately. It considered the first six months of 1973 as already covered, except over consumable supplies and plant operation. Its comparative budget for one school year was for July 1973 to June 1974. Additional needs could be hidden in the extraneous needs for the rest of the existing school year. Wellesley also decided to move to the fiscal year. The six months were an addition to the present academic year. Weston did the most complete analysis by providing data on each of the six months. Its basic point of comparison like Quincy's was the calendar year 1973. In fact these technical methods did not have a differential impact upon total budget requests. In Quincy and Melrose the usual 5 percent nonsalary increase was apparently reduced to *zero* for one year, calendar or academic. In Wellesley and Weston the 10 percent nonsalary increase was ostensibly reduced to about 5 percent to be in line with inflation. All four intended to maintain the status quo net of national inflation of 4 percent. Declining enrollments in all four districts were said to be important in achieving this, even though the changes were not even throughout the schools.

PREDICTED COMMITTEE REACTIONS

The main consideration, then, was committee reactions. The general issues were similar. Few innovations were proposed. Plant or program renewal was at a minimum. Only necessary consumable spending was retained. The main problem of inflationary increase was said to be plant operation or reapirs. The superintendents wanted to steer the committees away from consideration of the instructional programs. How they did so depended upon their evaluation of the committee, whether they saw it as an ally or an adversary.

Quincy was unique in viewing its committee cautiously. This was a new view. The superintendent had experienced a great change in behavior from supportive and acquiescent to suspicious and interrogative. He saw this new committee, in office since January 1971, mainly as an adversary:

> Increasingly I see the committee as my adversary. That was not the case with the former school committee. . . . They were on for a different purpose—a president of the local college, and a stockbroker. They would not dirty their hands to be on the city council.[28]

He tried to ensure that the most quizzical member—a former city councillor—could not find fault with his management of the system: "Our offensive was keyed to McCauley. By being able to answer him we would overkill on everyone else."[29] He also made several moves on specific items for this member:

> McCauley knows that the research assistant at North Quincy High has moved from here and so the job is running light. We're only carrying one vacancy but we need to hide the fact for we need these places. . . . But I'm not going to ask for anything I can't justify. I just want to hold on to what I've got.[30]

He was cautious of other members and, for example, cut out increases in research development. He also avoided implementation of the state-mandated elementary lunch program: it had originally caused controversy. On the other hand, against his own judgment he included one small plant renovation, at the special request of one member. He predicted it would be cut by another:

> SUPERINTENDENT: What is this building request?
> DIRECTOR OF PLANT: A good part of it is Davis' request for paving the Merrimount tennis court.
> COORDINATOR: It is not one of our priorities. The kids won't use it.
> SUPERINTENDENT: Ask the principal for a report and then in the meeting we can role play with McCauley and show from the report that the kids won't use it. I'll say it's not an issue with the PTA.[31]

He deliberately put in money for community use of plant, saying, "This will be of great interest to Davis. . . ."

The Melrose superintendent was also careful not to include items that might cause controversy with the committee. He cut down administrative out-of-state travel allowances. Many members had been outraged at that abuse by city aldermen. He would not include the chairman's special request of a heart machine. The previous year, the aldermen had insisted on its deletion. The superintendent was concerned by his situation, although he regarded the committee colleagially: "I predict a lot of fuming this year especially over salary and the 18 months so I'm going to be careful to prune. . . ."[32]

The Wellesley superintendent had a less easy task than in Melrose. His committee was made up of quarrelsome members. He still felt that they were allies. He tried to present a budget that he and his staff had found desirable within his guidelines. He used business methods and did not obviously favor any particular instructional program but he was chary:

> I believe the school committee could rubber stamp my proposed budget, but because of the Town Meeting it must go through a transformation from mine to the committee's. Also there is the New England distrust of administrators that I've got to contend with. . . .[33]

The Weston superintendent saw his committee as colleagial, but he had to cut some improvements he wanted, such as teacher aides. He knew that the committee chairman was totally opposed. He also avoided equipment increases since his members had expressed strong feelings.

SUPERINTENDENT PROFESSIONAL IMAGES

The planned committee focus on items other than instruction was because of the superintendents' view of their own roles versus the committees'. The Quincy superintendent was clearest on this:

> I don't want the school committee to do anything to the instructional program but I'll tell them they are the custodians of the buildings and can decide whether to keep it in good condition or not. . . . As regards this program there is no point in clouding the issue with facts. . . .[34]

All viewed themselves primarily as experts in education or instructional leaders of the school system. Their main concern was to protect these interests. Again, methods varied. The Quincy and Melrose superintendents saw themselves first and foremost as educational leaders, involved in implementing their own particular policies. They were willing to relinquish responsibility for technical, non-educational matters such as plant operation. The Wellesley superintendent saw himself more as a general manager and not personally committed to a program. Weston's superintendent was more equivocal but more a manager than educator per se.

These views affected, for example, who would be involved in budget presentation. It was seen as a skilled exercise, for which colleagues were trained or excluded. In Quincy, therefore, a dress rehearsal was held. The superintendent stressed the "scientific" nature of the process, adding to his LMT and IPT:

> I want to go in there with a high degree of credibility. I may ask you to present your parts of the budget. But there is a science to it and I don't know whether you know it. So I may do it myself.[35]

The other superintendents were also wary about presenting their information to committee. They, too, tried to simplify the data and had a clear view of the importance of their own role. They also controlled the involvement of administrators and teachers with the committee.

Administrators did not usually present budget proposals to the committees. The superintendent acted as spokesman. The majority of the 10 administrators interviewed in the four school districts saw this as right and proper. They would only present their cases if asked and if necessary. They did not want to burden the superintendent with defending their work which required detailed knowledge, but they would not circumvent the superintendent to the committee. As a principal said, "It is not protocol."[36]

The Melrose superintendent was as rigid as in Quincy; the chairman of debates asked him for permission to speak to the meeting. The reply was: "I will not allow pressure tactics. Give me your statement and I'll present it to the committee."[37] In fact, many Melrose administrators did not know the school committee members. The principal of the junior high school said:

> I haven't been asked to go to the committee. The superintendent does it himself—we talk with him and he is our spokesman. He sees it as that. It takes too much of our time. I appreciate his concern. I am prepared to go if called. I never have been and I don't know most of the committee members. . . . It's not like my old school committee. . . .[38]

On the other hand, the superintendents did not necessarily see it as their responsibility to speak for the entire system. In Quincy and Melrose where the superintendents were firm educators, they allowed technical administrators to speak to their own tasks. In Wellesley and Weston where the superintendents were more concerned to balance out all interests more administrators, both technical and instructional were allowed to speak to the committees. Weston's superintendent allowed his business assistant to present the financial aspects and the two program directors to speak to their work. He would present a comprehensive, but brief, review.

The superintendents made determined efforts to simplify the information on which the committees would make their decisions. They did so not only recognizing that the committees would not have sufficient time to scrutinize budgets but also because they wished to avoid confrontation on educational policy. They therefore focused on items they did not think they should, or did not wish to, control. The Melrose superintendent was adamant about this:

> I don't think the committee should be given all the information for they are part-timers and I am working full-time. I don't know what they do all day and by analogy they cannot know what I do. So the committee should trust my judgment and let me make the decisions.[39]

The superintendents had clear views of their professional tasks. They were not merely the result of a necessary division of labor in a complex and busy society but were special tasks requiring expert rather than lay knowledge.

SUMMARY

The preparation of the budget is achieved by the professional educators, clearly directed by the superintendent. His approach is conditioned by his own evaluation of community needs and demands. The teachers and administrators are involved in their work capacity rather than as a professional organization. The teacher associations, for example, played no part in this stage of the process. This method affected the cohesiveness of the profession. Community input is also indirect: it is felt only through pressure group tactics. Needs are aggregated and ranked by the superintendents. There is no systematic method of determining priorities. They are reached by an intuitive, but professional, judgment of likely committee wishes and responses. It is to the responses that we now turn.

NOTES TO CHAPTER FOUR

1. For a full discussion of the differences between conscious and unconscious decisions, see Karl Deutsch, *Nerves of Government* (New York: Free Press, 1963) and the point developed by P. Bachrach and M. Baratz, *Power and Poverty: Theory and Practice* (London: Oxford University Press, 1970), ch. 7.
2. *Melrose Ordinances,* revised 1956: Title 3, section 19.
3. General Laws of the State of Massachusetts, 1972.
4. Wellesley school committee's policy rules book, 1973.
5. Annual Report for Weston Schools, 1971.
6. Information from the superintendents and their staff, October 1972 through January 1973.
7. Interview with Ms. Joan Wexler, February 19, 1973, in Weston.
8. Interview with Dr. Creedon, *op. cit.*
9. A term used initially by the respondents in interviews rather than a cate-

gory for an answer to a question of mine. I started by using the same categories as Neal Gross in *Explorations in Role Analysis* (New York: Wiley, 1958), p. 239.

10. From interviews with 26 school committee members, January to February 1973.
11. Election campaigns for state offices, 1972, and reported in interviews, *ibid.*
12. Interview with Dr. Wood, *op. cit.*
13. Reported in the *Patriot Ledger,* Quincy, March 1973.
14. The preliminary school budget, presented to the Wellesley school committee in November 1972, p. 1.
15. Reported in the *Patriot Ledger,* Quincy, on January 5, 1972.
16. Interview with Walter Hannon, *op. cit.*
17. Meeting on October 11, 1972, in Melrose.
18. Report of the Town Meeting, March 1971.
19. Memorandum from Leo Turo, Massachusetts State Department of Education, Bureau of School Management, November 21, 1972.
20. H. T. James, *The School Budgetary Process in Large Cities.* In A. Rosenthal (ed.), *Governing Education* (Garden City: Doubleday, 1969) p. 338.
21. This notion is developed more fully in my forthcoming work on the English educational system. M.E. David and M.H. Peston, *Planning Educational Change* (London: Athlone Press, 1975).
22. Annual Report of Quincy Schools, 1971, p. 3.
23. Internal Memorandum from Dr. Goodman, October 1972.
24. Internal Memorandum to Quincy's committee, November 23, 1972.
25. November 20, 1972 in Quincy's committee rooms.
26. In 1972 it was $64.34 and for 1973–4 revised to $66.06 for 16,500 pupils.
27. Meetings of October-November 1972 in Melrose.
28. Interview with Dr. L. Creedon, December 21, 1972, in Quincy.
29. *Ibid.*
30. *Ibid.*
31. LMT meeting in Quincy, November 9, 1972.
32. Interview with Dr. Quin, Melrose, *op. cit.*
33. Interview with Dr. Goodman, Wellesley, *op. cit.*
34. LMT Meeting, *op. cit.*
35. *Ibid.*
36. Interview with Mr. Ted Rockicki, Wellesley, January 16, 1973.
37. An administrative meeting in Melrose, November 10, 1972.
38. Interview with Mr. Ed. Barry, Melrose, January 12, 1973.
39. Dr. Quin, *op. cit.*

Chapter Five

Committee Deliberations on Budget Proposals

This chapter presents a discussion on how the school committees dealt with the proposals for the operating budget. The reactions of the members are analyzed in terms of their motives as public officials. An assessment of the variations in behavior is made, with size used as the crucial explanatory variable. Other factors such as political attitudes and culture are also reviewed. They all help explain method and style of debates. Budget outcomes are virtually unchanged from the superintendent proposals.

In summary, the school committees all used the same basic strategy. They asked questions on the information set before them. The ways in which they reviewed the data varied from convivial and colleagial to hostile and antagonistic. All the members saw it as proper that the superintendent present them with basic data to begin their review. They waited for the superintendent to present them with a budget which he could live with for the next year and which he could define in terms of its legitimacy and adequacy.[1] Here review questions differed. Some members felt that they should provide support for the professional educators' work; others thought that they should ensure that the professional educators were "honest and not trying to run a loose ship."[2]

Although the basic approach was the same, the substance of the process varied. First, the circumstances affected necessary changes. Second, and more important, the superintendents asked the committees to focus on particular issues in distinctive ways. The 18-month budget added a complication. The main point is that the superintendents chose what and how it would be considered. They set the boundaries of the budget issues by simplifying problems and focusing attention mainly upon programs other than instruction. They held firm notions of the controllable and discretionary issues. They directed their committees to these by use of budget booklets, agendas for meetings, and their own colleagues.

SCOPE OF BUDGET CONSIDERATION

The superintendents had one major limitation on the proposals they presented: they were not entirely free to construct the budget. It was not for them to determine salary with the professional employees. This was a real constraint since the salary bill constituted the largest single expenditure. However, the committees did not feel it was an important issue or one that impinged upon the operating budget. It was merely the salary increase that was a separate matter of debate. The superintendents still had responsibility for recommending personnel numbers in various categories that they would need to run their school system. But the total number was clearly dependent upon available money to pay them. The superintendents had as much idea as the committees of the range of possible increase that could be negotiated. They could judge the consequent size of the non-salary, operating budget.

SUPERINTENDENT STRATEGIES

There were many strategies they could use for substantive review. They could start with the figure for the total budget and its increase over the previous year. They could get approval for its sufficiency before looking at the component programs. Alternatively, they could focus upon the elements of the budget and consider the adequacy of each program within the school system. The increase in the total budget would be reviewed with reference to its constituent parts. Given the economic situation, the 18-month budget, and the separate review of salary increase, the tactics used were similar. The superintendents briefly reviewed the essential instructional program. They then pointed to the potential reasons for inflationary increases.

Three superintendents totally ignored treatment of salary, taking it as a separate issue. They did not key their presentations to an important comparison between years, because of the 18-month complication. They emphasized their efforts to contain budget increases within particular categories of spending.

In Quincy the review started before the entire budget had been constructed. Three booklets were eventually produced. The superintendent asked the school committee to analyze the operating budget for instructional supplies and plant operation, without the salary budget, new programs, or the budget for the Quincy Junior College.[3] In fact, the latter was self-sufficient but did operate at an estimated cost of $1,314,119 for the 18-months.[4] The reason given for this tactic of presenting separate budget books and putting emphasis primarily on non-salary costs was that, "This is where we put the lion's share of work."[5] Members had to consider proposed expenditures in terms of different resources over all programs and by annual comparison.

In Melrose, the recent strategy of presenting the entire budget in one booklet was used. The committee was asked to consider expenses for plant, instructional, and athletics programs before the personnel budget.[6] The salary bill was constructed separately. A booklet was constructed for the whole Wellesley budget, too. The superintendent asked the committee to consider the merits of each program in terms of all resources—expense, plant, and personnel.[7] This was a new approach derived from the consultants. It was program budgeting, and substantially different from Quincy and Melrose.

But it was only in Weston that tactics were very distinctive. The superintendent first asked the committee to consider the budget total—salary and expenses—and pronounce on the adequacy of increase.[8] Then the contents would be reviewed. There are two clear reasons for diversity of appraisal. First, the custom in Weston had been to consider a tentative budget in the December, three months before the town meeting, to give the town comptroller an idea of the proposed total. This operation was rather meaningless, but was ritualistically conducted.[9] In December of 1972 the school committee approved an estimated 12 percent increase for 1973 over 1972. This budget was not detailed. The superintendent then worked on his review.

Secondly, Weston's salary negotiations usually began in January. Although the superintendent was no more involved than the other three, he was concerned about the proportion of budget increase devoted to teachers' salaries. He felt unable to administer the school program adequately. He did not have enough resources from the budget once salary had been apportioned.[10] The traditional Weston priority was to pay teachers well, to attract the best qualified people, and to compete with neighboring or wealthy school districts.[11] The superintendent merely pointed out his dilemma to his committee. He then proceeded like the other three to get his committee to consider the composite elements.

Size may have been the reason for Weston superintendent's primarily distinctive tactics. But the Wellesley and Melrose superintendents claimed that their budget tactic was for them a unique circumstance. Usually they have to consider the possible salary increase. The previous year the committees had both spent longer than ever before in bargaining with the teachers. The final outcome was that they had settled on a two-year contract, containing two cost of living increases. The two teacher associations had agreed the contract because of their predictions of national and local inflation. Negotiations were conditioned by national wage and price controls, imposed in 1970 and which, by the summer of 1972, were likely to be effective for several years.[12] The contracts were found acceptable at the end of a long and bitter process of bargaining. Teacher negotiations usually have a strong effect on budget review. The superintendent in Wellesley, for example, said, "The number-one effect on the school budget, teacher morale, and town and gown relations is negotiations."[13] It may be that there is usually no difference among these three districts.

Quincy had not completed negotiations with its teachers for 1973–74. Yet it did not discuss the issue with the operating budget. Separate, private sessions were held to consider a collective bargaining strategy. They agreed to submit the existing salary contracts [14] in the budget if they did not reach agreement with the teachers before March 1973. This was the statutory date for the sub.nission to the mayor for inclusion in the tax rate. They would ask for a separate allocation to cover the negotiated increase when the contracts were settled.

Quincy and Weston's tactics may be associated with their differential wealth. This has consequences for the esteem held for teachers. A mediating factor may be the political culture, the values of the community expressed through the political process, rather than size. It seems most plausible that Weston was concerned about salary because it could afford to spend money on teachers. Wellesley had been in a similar position until the last few years. Quincy did not have a strong enough tax base to be lavish in salary settlements. Melrose had also always been frugal with its salary scales, given its poorer tax base. Size does not seem to be the sole criterion of the different budgetary approaches.[15]

SUPERINTENDENT PRIORITIES

Apart from salary and its relation to the budget total, the superintendents adopted similar strategies, which stemmed from their professionalism. They all made efforts to avoid confrontations on the educational issues, although the Wellesley superintendent was the least directive.

The actual strategies were the following. In Quincy the superintendent gave a long budget presentation, discussing expense items.[16] He wanted the committee to compare similar resources across the system and not "item by item, page by page."[17] The budget booklet had not been formulated to aid this since the budget preparation had been constrained by existing and state accounting practices. The superintendent also tried to get immediate committee approval to the expense budget. He showed that he had cut $3,568 for the calendar year 1973 over 1972; in fact, 0.1 percent in a $3½ million budget. It was because:

> . . . of economies made as a result of program budgeting and a decrease in student enrollments over the last year. I also have not included an inflationary factor of 3–4%. If it were included the budget would be $100,000 to $140,000 more.[18]

He stressed that the largest increase was in uncontrollable areas—plant operation and state programs. The implication was that the instructional programs were tight. Since the committee did not endorse this, he presented a schedule for budget consideration in which he would provide the explanations.

In Melrose, the superintendent gave little verbal presentation, for he had written a summary of his recommendations. He, too, stressed his attempts to keep the equivalent calendar year expense items the same, indicating, in fact, a cutback. He explained it in terms of declining elementary school enrollments: 0.3 percent. He also made much of the inflationary cost of plant operation. He added:

> The general practice has been to leave things in the budget for school committee to take action on. This is time consuming and often means that they are making decisions on things they know hardly anything about. So this year, given the economic situation, I presented a 'tight' budget.[19]

The superintendent in Wellesley did not present a long, verbal summary of his budget in public. He, too, gave members a written statement of the budget and its assumptions.[20] He had the added complications of explaining the program format and the 18-month issue. Each of the 50 programs had to be inspected against a statement of goals. To ease matters, the booklet contained a summary of the traditional budget. He did not give a criterion of evaluation, since he expected subjective judgments. To this end, he called in administrators to explain proposed program changes. The first open budget meeting was devoted to this exercise.[21] The focus was on system developments rather than the cost burden.

The Weston committee, like that in Quincy and Melrose, was asked to look at the large and inflationary costs of plant operation. There was no written summary but a verbal presentation.[22] The superintendent and program directors focused on changes to achieve savings and commensurate improvements. Even so, the nonsalary budget had increased 2.7 percent for the calendar year 1973 over 1972. Personnel changes would only effect a 0.4 percent reduction on 1972. The superintendent also evaluated teacher performance in programs.

TIME SPENT ON SCHOOL COMMITTEE REVIEW

The school committees reviewed the budget as asked. On the whole, they did not raise other issues. Not that they did not spend much time on review, but the time spent related to finding out how the system worked and deciding on the adequacy or viability of proposed changes.

Because issues varied, time spent varied, as Table 5-1 shows.[23] Quincy reviewed over three months and held 12 meetings, each over three hours in duration. Melrose spent almost two months and held nine three-hour meetings. Wellesley reviewed for two and a half months, and held six open and at least three closed meetings. Weston held seven, including two closed sessions, over a five-week period. Time spent is a weak criterion of involvement,

Table 5-1. Time Spent on Review

Municipality	No. of Committee Members	Budget Meetings	No. of Schools
Weston	5	7	6
Wellesley	5	9	10
Melrose	9	9	14
Quincy	7	12	30

Source: Information from the four superintendents.

but it is related to size. Size obviously affects the division of labor, given similar committee—and different community—size. More time spent does not, therefore, imply more intimate involvement with the individual schools and programs. Quincy's discussions may also have been protracted because of committee inter-action, that is, the degree of conflict or consensus among members. Wellesley perhaps held more budget meetings than Melrose; several were in private session due to the fact that its members did not reach an easy consensus. Committee interaction as an explanation will merit further exploration.

CONTENT OF COMMITTEE REVIEWS

In three the predominant debate centered on issues peripheral to the main instructional program, although every item was cursorily inspected. The discus-sions mainly related to plant operation and to issues such as athletics or the state lunch program. In other words, the issues were at the margins of the school system rather than its fundamentals. There were clear enough reasons for this. This was what the superintendents had aimed for. They wanted the discussions to be on the least sensitive issues, either educationally or politically. They wanted to control instructional matters to their own satisfaction. The superintendents were not able to predict with complete accuracy the medium of debate or committee interaction, but they were able to direct the course of events along certain lines.

In Quincy, all the discussions were long and acrimonious. On the whole, the questions directly related to business matters such as transportation contracts or provision for student safety at a high school. Indeed, one entire meeting consisted of a vituperative argument about the use of a walkway between high schools. The argument really was about the educators' and poli-ticians' roles as public officials. The mayor, who started the argument, did not want to appear a public "jerk" for overprotecting the children.[24] The superintendent, in response, was vehemently concerned to ensure the adequate safety of all school children. He felt that this was his proper responsibility. The obvious discrepancy in role definition in this case was settled in favor of the superintendent.

The committee also considered public communication. One member felt that a local publication was costly, inefficient, and ineffective.[25] He succeeded in reducing the allocation. The other concerns were whether to implement the state lunch program, how best to present the 18-month budget, whether to pay for the athletic uniforms of the color guard.

One new member tried to reduce the per pupil formula for instructional supplies. This aroused angry and heated responses from the older committee members and the senior administrators. It was seen as an infringement of administrative rights or professional duties and was quickly dismissed as a topic of debate. The new member was chided for straying into an academic area. The superintendent used his professional educators to put his case more strongly. He and the older members had a clear notion of his and the committee's roles.

The superintendent successfully maintained full control over the instructional programs. He and his senior administrators felt it was their right to do so. Indeed the superintendent was subsequently upset about his angry exchange with the mayor.[26] He claimed that he should not have mentioned the item, that he had made a mistake. It would have been proper for him to have avoided such a controversy by not informing the committee of the real contents of the item. This was an area for his personal influence. The debates in Quincy illustrate the problems of reaching adequate and workable definitions of professional versus political expertise.

In Melrose the debate was not as detailed or bitter. Mostly it centered on plant operation, high school equipment, and snow removal. The latter was discussed over three meetings. Other topics were art equipment, the athletics program, and the merits and disadvantages of the rifle and cross-country programs. There was almost no discussion of the instructional programs. Staffing was barely mentioned. Although the superintendent presented a brief analysis, he argued that until more was known of actual resignations, discussion was not pertinent. Policies for sabbatical leaves and teacher aides amended by the superintendent were not covered. Nor was the pupil-teacher ratio. The superintendent was able to direct the instructional programs according to his professional judgment. The changes made in the system were peripheral to these programs.

Another major issue was presenting the 18-month budget. One member was concerned about the effect on the tax rate of teachers' salaries. In particular the summer months' payments of 1974 were an added burden. He tried to make political capital, claiming that these did not properly pertain to the fiscal year 1974. If he could obtain legal sanction not to encumber them in this budget he could effect "a saving of over a million dollars to Melrose and $100 million to Massachusetts—and over $2 on the Melrose tax rate."[27]

He thus formulated for the State Legislature a bill to make this deferment legal. The rest of the committee refused to endorse the bill officially, though they agreed to a personal submission with the superintendent's support.

The areas of debate were clear. The committee concentrated on technical and political rather than substantive educational problems. In this case harmony rather than internal conflict was the predominant style of debate.

The Weston committee, like that in Quincy and Melrose, stuck closely to the superintendent's suggested strategy. The members first considered plant operation, then expense items, and finally program changes relating to staff reallocations between the four elementary schools for music and physical education, and between the high schools. The staff proposal would require drastic changes to the instructional program at the junior high school. For the time being, the proposals related only to a reduction of high school foreign languages. There was little explicit demand for them, using pupil-teacher ratios as an indicator. The superintendent presented a long analysis and alternate strategy. The committee found his views acceptable since they were based on discussions with the relevant professional educators. The review was mainly rapid scrutiny of equipment and supplies by comparison with previous years. The members did not make any changes, except for the removal of a large item of equipment—for the high school gym—from which the superintendent withdrew his tentative support. They found the item easily because of the array of statistical information. The operating and supplies budget was not very lavish. The main debate was over a strategy for salary negotiations. The rest of the review was accomplished in a very short time, relying on the superintendent's expertise. Although judgments were made of the instructional program, they were made at the superintendent's behest and were mere affirmation.

In Wellesley the school committee was less subservient. This was partly because the superintendent was less directive, and partly due to the peculiar situation. The school committee was expected to perform a new evaluation of programs rather than items of expenditure. The members did not know how best to do this. They could not go through the budget line by line. One member remarked:

> We did not go through page by page because we did not want to knitpick. . . . This year I was more willing to take a meataxe approach because it was obviously a difficult year.[28]

Some members were concerned about the total increase. They felt that particular committee policies affected this. They asked for business changes especially in elementary schools policy to reduce the increase. Aspects of the neighborhood policy had been discussed periodically in the last few years.[29] They had not been settled to the satisfaction of all the committee members.[30] The issues were whether to close an elementary school, in view of declining enrollments and the age of buildings; whether to implement the state lunch program; whether to have double or single kindergarten sessions. The members felt that the neighborhood policy was becoming too costly to administer, given the schools' location and condition and spread of pupils. It was probably irrelevant to parental wishes. They raised these new issues rather than inspecting those of the superintendent.

They also addressed three business issues highlighted by the budget—transportation, lunch program, and plant operation. The main review, however, was of the neighborhood policy: not its educational merits but its costs. All the changes mooted were to save money. Only subsequently were they justified as being educationally preferable. The members did not feel convinced of their stand. They asked the superintendent for his advice and recommendations, and eventually did not proceed without it.

The eventual budget review was very brief because the committee spent almost two months debating the elementary policy. It had not inspected any other programs. When it did so, it demanded more information by which to judge the system's workings. Some members wanted lists of equipment (which were automatically provided in the three other areas) and personnel. The superintendent had deliberately not provided them, viewing it as unnecessary and pertaining to what he called administration rather than policy.[31] In his three and a half years as superintendent, he had been at pains to teach his committee about that proper divide. On request he produced the lists, but the committee then decided he should have full responsibility for them and should use his discretion to remove low priority items of equipment.

The members themselves also reduced capital outlay for educational "frills," namely, the curriculum center, summer workshops, and plant renovation. The main debate was of these frills, and items peripheral to the essential workings of the system. The committee touched on educational priorities but finally left it to the superintendent to decide on them. In the last analysis, the superintendent was responsible for budget changes, reductions affecting the system's workings. The members, too, had a notion of professional tasks. They had not relied on them primarily, but had tried to change the definition of the situation. This was without lasting effect.

REVIEW METHODS

The budget reviews were disparate in time spent and in content. The method of review also differed. Three committees went through the budget books conventionally—"page by page: item by item."[32] In Quincy there was the most direct straight-line approach—the members were questioned on each item as they went through the book. In Melrose, the members jumped from topic to topic as directed there by the superintendent and by use of the professional, technical administrators. In Weston, after general discussion, the committee thumbed through the book, looking at the statistics of items as "targets of opportunity."[33] They did use the four senior administrators when necessary, for they attended all the meetings.

It was only in Wellesley that the books were hardly opened. The members did not inspect each of the programs and the resources. They talked more globally, mainly about the neighborhood policy. They had the senior administrators available for advice. They avoided learning about program evaluation because it was new.

The members focused on issues that seemed pertinent to one of them or were capable of immediate resolution. They looked for extraordinary problems rather than reviewing the adequacy or legitimacy of the regular school programs. They did not compare performance or provision with other towns or cities. They focused mainly on the non-essential items which could be deemed to be controversial—whether or not to buy a piece of equipment, whether to implement a program not of their own choosing, and so on. They also focused on issues of immediate consequence to their own political careers—how to present the 18-month budget so that the increase in tax rate would not appear large in comparison with the previous year. It was this issue that they reckoned would be the most publicly recognized. They did not want to appear to be "feckless spenders without consideration to the community's ability to pay."[34]

ATTITUDES TOWARD BUDGET REVIEW

Most members interviewed felt that the budget approach they adopted was adequate. The definition of two separate budget issues—operating and salary— was an appropriate allocation of work. They accepted the superintendent's definition of their tasks and did not try to consider the two aspects together. As regards the operating budget strategy, one member said: "We can't have an objective analysis. It must be done by subtle osmosis."[35] As the superintendent directed them, so they concurred. They either compared years or looked for large items of expenditure. Another member explained this procedure as this: "It is easiest to focus on capital outlay."[36]

Although the members felt that many areas of the budget were set, such as personnel, instructional programs and state programs, they still felt free to choose the budget and policy changes they desired.[37] They were not compelled to certain issues, and could examine sacred cows if they wished. It was only Weston's members that would have preferred a full program analysis and evaluation rather than that the ad hoc and random target shots. The majority of members were satisfied with their achievements. Although the salary settlement was seen as a constraint on review, few members wanted to pursue personnel matters in more detail. They felt that they should review the numerous issues set before them.

Few members advocated an alternate review or more drastic changes.[38] The chairman of Wellesley said:

Being realistic, it is very hard to eliminate programs. There is the

problem of demand by youngsters and the college board exams.
But I'd put the emphasis on research and development to improve the system.[39]

They could not be rational or systematic. The superintendent's work was adequate for the majority and the information sufficient for decisions. The criticisms
were at the margins, and the predominant view was of an adequate school
administration.[40]

EFFECTS ON BUDGET OUTCOMES

Although satisfied, the budget reviews did not accomplish much. The superintendents' recommendations were barely altered. The most change occurred
in Wellesley—almost 10 percent of the proposed total was removed in reducing
equipment, summer workshops, and plant renovation.[41] The committee's
first priority, to revise the neighborhood policy, was not achieved. The result
was that the committee agreed to implement the state-mandated lunch program.
Staffing and the educational programs remained unaltered.

In the other three districts, only small changes were made. In
Quincy the changes were minimal—$130,000 out of a $31 million budget—to
reduce the frequency of the newsheet publication, to cut down on plant renovations, to change the transport contract, to cut out two teaching vacancies,
one research assistant post, and the athletics uniforms.[42] What the members
finally did include, after four tablings of the motion not to, was the state lunch
program. They also did make certain changes over the 18-month budget. Many
other changes were proposed, but the status quo eventually remained. The
superintendent did have to concede a new business practice over the 18-month
budget, but not in the area he cared most about. He was jubilant that "not a
dime has been cut from the instructional program. It never has in my five years
as superintendent."[43]

The Melrose committee effected few changes. It wanted to achieve
two—to abolish the rifle team and to reduce the tax burden of the 18-month
transition—but neither was successful. After initial budget approval, the committee did reduce the total by under 1 percent under external pressure and
with some staff changes. On the other hand, as a result of an administrative
error, two small programs were added. The overall changes in the $11 million
budget were slight.

The Weston committee was not keen to achieve major reductions,
perhaps because budget changes had been agreed colleagially, before presentation of the proposals. The members reinstated more than they removed. They
accepted the case for the retention of the foreign language programs. They only
removed one item of equipment. The final budgets are shown in Table 5-2.

The differences observed had to do with process, not outcome.

Table 5-2.   Budget Appropriation for 1973-4

	Salaries	Expenses	Total
Quincy	$26,095,813*	$5,593,630	$32,923,095
Melrose	10,720,160	1,237,352	11,957,512
Wellesley	12,183,420	2,437,789	14,621,209
Weston	6,615,622	1,130,471	7,746,093

*Regular schools only, i.e., excludes Quincy Junior College, and does not include food services.

Source: Information presented at the public hearings in each district.

Yet they require explanation. The patterning is not around the issue of size, as was predicted.

REASONS FOR DIFFERENT BEHAVIOR

The committees generally accepted what was put before them and only argued on the margins of the system. Differences concerned method and style of debate. Substance of review was a result of the superintendents' definitions of important issues. This was because there is agreement between school committee members and superintendents on the nature and boundaries of their roles. Administrative style, however, does not explain method or style of debate. The observed differences in committee behavior and interaction also do not seem to be related to size. There were differences between Wellesley, Melrose, and Weston as well as between Weston and Quincy. Indeed, the basic similarities are between the larger city and town and the smaller town and city. In Wellesley and Quincy the interaction was based on conflict; in Weston and Melrose, concensus. Wealth is also an inadequate explanation since Wellesley and Weston differ.

The substance of debate varies but around an agreed view of legitimate areas of intervention. Style and method vary because of the actual attitudes of committee members, towards political office and the consequent committee interaction. This was partly mediated by the chairmen. These attitudes generally stem from type of political commitment.

COMMITTEE ROLE:
THE MEMBERS' PERCEPTIONS

The members interviewed all had strong views about their mode of behavior over the budget and policy-making. These related to their notions of the superintendent's role which fit in with the superintendents' own definitions. The members defined their role on the committee as the "trustees of the school system."[44] They added that the "input comes from the administration."

The role of the committee member is to be devil's advocate, to ask questions and review superintendent recommendations.[45] One member jocularly said, "The superintendent recommends; the committee votes."[46] This, in fact, was a fairly accurate description of the situation. The members checked the adequacy of the system by going through the superintendents' recommendations.

The members' attitudes to the superintendent role were not contradictory. They should not interfere with what he had defined as his own work: "It is not proper for us to originate policy. We have to react to the superintendent. We are not geared to initiating policy."[47] If budget changes were necessary, for example, the committee should rely on the superintendent's advice. Moreover, they had clear views of where they could or should not intervene. One member put it simply: "We leave the academic end to the professional educators."[48]

The superintendent's role could be clearly articulated. He is the professional and educational leader of the system. Again one member expressed it succinctly:

> The superintendent's role should be to stand head and shoulders over the community as educational leader and inspiration, to be sights ahead of everyone else, and to set the tone and quality for educational excellence. In other words, he should be concerned with efficiency and not be scholarly. He should be pushing people without making them aware. He should be a good judge of people. . . . He's an ivory tower approach. . . .[49]

But they saw him not only as the educational leader but also as a political one. The majority were willing to fire a superintendent if his leadership were not in line with their thinking. The superintendent should not only act on his educational expertise but should also be a funnel or filter of information. This was necessary since the members themselves did not have time to synthesize all the information in the system. Educational expertise was not the only criterion by which to judge a superintendent. Business and committee management were also important.

The superintendent was, after all, the committee's employee and chief executive. Although his advice was regarded as needed for committee decisions, it was not necessarily sufficient, and uncontrovertible:

> I listened to the superintendent—this is his work—the budget. . . . I need experts. . . . I am not an educator. . . But a lot of it is also common sense. . . . I don't need the superintendent to tell me about the front-end loader. . . .[50]

The members, therefore, distinguish between educational expertise and technical or business competence. The prime evaluation of a superintendent is his academic expertise. Members can intervene in non-academic, political or business matters such as whether to buy a vehicle for snow removal.

REASONS FOR HOLDING POLITICAL OFFICE

Although the members concurred on definition of roles and their boundaries, actual role behavior varied according to political motivation. Some members saw the superintendent as an adversary whose ideas should be challenged and queried. The superintendent should be able to present a defense and justification for what he was doing. The model of the *judicial* system was used as the basis for this approach:

> My role in the budget is basically the same as that of any school committee in the American political set up. We are the sounding board for the community. We reflect people's ideas through the budgetary process. It is ironic that the superintendent is put in an adversary position and it is rather gruesome. But I'm the voice of the people . . . to ask the questions. A sort of scrutiny by homeowners . . . it's a game.[51]

Other members took a different tack. The superintendent was their ally and colleague. They did not try to open up the system. They used the model of *business management* to define their strategy.[52] In this case the superintendent was the managing director who had a working knowledge of the system. The purpose of a school committee was as a check on the administration: "They sometimes get too close to the system."[53]

The Weston chairman eloquently specified this position:

> My job is to review the budget recommendations of the superintendent and try to determine consistency with educational objectives of the town in terms of dollars. I especially try to
> a. avoid larger increases than are necessary
> b. supervise the administration
> c. check whether it is careful and thorough work
> d. ask enough questions to understand what is going on
> e. make myself familiar with the budget to present it to the town
> f. manage the system to accommodate the spectrum of opinion. . . .[54]

These strategic models derive from attitudes to public service. Gross's (1958) analysis of the role of members relied on three categories of classification.[55] These were civic duty, representing a particular group or set of opinions, and political ambition. The three categories are not appropriate to these data on the four school districts. None of the 26 admitted political ambition, other than being a school official.[56] Many members did serve out of civic duty. This too broad to discriminate between actual opinions. Few members were willing to state categorically any partisan representation. Given that all members are elected at large, they do not have a geographical constituency. The official notion of non-partisan committees precludes admittance of a group loyalty.

The basic differences are between those who stand on a "fiscally responsible" slate and those who serve "educational interests."[57] The former try to cut costs of education. They regard themselves as representative of the homeowner and politically conservative, the majority of local citizens. The latter try to improve the system by relying basically on means presented by the administration. They represent current parental concern. These attitudes are not obviously linked to the traditional dichotomy of left and right politics.

A concern with costs led to the adversary mode of behavior, most manifest in Quincy and Wellesley,[58] as shown in Table 5-3. A minority of Melrose members had a similar attitude, but it was not manifest in Melrose's committee. A concern with education led to a more supportive and colleagial mode of behavior with the superintendent. This was observed in both Melrose and Weston.

In Quincy, for example, the overall method was to go through the budget with a fine-tooth comb.[59] The members mainly saw their job as paring down recommendations. They had to check that the superintendent had presented only what was absolutely necessary. The questions that were posed were to "keep the system honest":

> We make the best effort to keep the system and administrators honest in their request for monies. We therefore hold down the bureaucracy for it is trying to run the show. I don't trust them. But it is difficult to second guess the superintendent so we aim to appoint a good one and hope he does a good job. So the questions are rather hit and miss.[60]

Table 5-3. Political Attitudes of School Committee Members

	Fiscal Responsibility	Educational Effectiveness	Total Members
Quincy	4	3	7
Melrose	2	6	9*
Wellesley	3	2	5
Weston	1	4	5

*One member not interviewed.
Source: Interview data.

In Wellesley a similar attitude prevailed:

> It is the nature of the beast. We try to find ways to pare down the budget.[61]

Melrose and Weston defined their task differently. It was to ensure that the superintendent had sufficient funds to run an adequate school system. They went through the recommendations, checking on the sufficiency of the programs.

COMMITTEE INTERACTION

School committees are expected to act as a body rather than as separate individuals. Thus the decisions that are made relate to the modus operandi that obtains in committee. If members do not all have the same values it may be difficult to reach agreement and act in concert. The committees do not operate by prior executive session of partisan groups. They work within the actual committee meetings. All four committees used a chairman to regulate differences of opinion and conduct proceedings. Thus there may be a second reason for the patterning of style of debate. The chairman's actions help to explain differences in committee interaction.

In both Melrose and Weston the finance chairman played a leading part. He personally acquainted himself with the budget but relied on the superintendent for advice and support. The debate was guided by the chairman who had been well trained by the professional educators. The Melrose finance chairman was in any event well versed in budgeting, working as an investment analyst. He therefore helped on the budget preparation:

> I did a lot more than set the policy. I spent a lot of time working on the figures . . . I like fooling around with numbers. It's also my responsibility to the committee. I'm rather upset others did not spend nearly as long as I did.[62]

The Weston chairman also had experience of budgeting in his private occupation. The task for these two chairmen was not arduous. The members of each committee behaved colleagially. They did not disagree strongly about the direction of the school system.

In Quincy and Wellesley the budget debate was less orderly both because each chairman was less directive and the members were not in agreement with each other. There was no caucus in either committee: the members tended to align for particular issues. It was difficult to predict how they would behave from one issue to the next. The chairmen did not try to pull the committees together. Both relied heavily on the superintendent for clarification and did not try to direct the committee's work.

The chairman in Quincy abdicated a lot of his responsibilities. He refused to relinquish his position—his by virtue of being mayor—to the vice-chairman. He had not had previous experience on the school committee. He even felt that "We're not really involved in the decision-making process."[63] He allowed another member, also new, to assume the role of inquisitor.

The chairman in Wellesley was also unwilling to direct matters. He often allowed the superintendent informally to guide the discussions:

> I am a strong believer in the hands-off policy. I hire a good person as superintendent and hold him responsible for pruning the budget. I never pretend to know how to run the schools. I am on the board of directors and chairman of it. . . . I am not even a member of management.[64]

He had à hard task to keep a consensus in committee, which was not always apparent to the public. He relied on informal procedures; vote-taking was an empty formality.

The chairman did play a vital part in the four school districts by helping to structure the consensus and style of debate. In two districts this was an easy task; in the others it was more difficult because of the internal, contradictory views of the superintendents' competencies and adequacy of the school system.

SUMMARY

The committees do rely on superintendent input to structure their reviews. They follow administrative directives, accepting the narrow, non-educational definition of their work. But the method and style of review, if not substance or outcome, vary according to member attitudes to public office. These attitudes are not a function of school district size. They are rather a result of community values or the political culture. Quincy and Wellesley committees, partly because of non-directive chairmanship, were hostile to the superintendent and pursued an adversary strategy, based on a judicial model. Weston and Melrose were colleagial and supportive, using a business management model. Wellesley's behavior was the most distinctive, for it positively questioned its superintendent's proposals. The reason for this lies outside committee interaction or superintendent strategy alone. It relates to community characteristics and involvement. It is to this aspect that I now turn.

NOTES TO CHAPTER FIVE

1. This expression was used most frequently by Mr. Francis X. McCauley of Quincy in the budget debate and personal interview on January 18, 1973.
2. This phrase was coined in interview by Mr. Ernest Murphy of Melrose on January 5, 1973.

3. The superintendent presented the first budget proposals to the Quincy school committee on November 24, 1972.
4. See details in unpublished booklet for 1973–74 Quincy budget, first presented in December 1972.
5. Superintendent's comment on November 24, 1972, and repeated at sub-sequent school committee meetings.
6. The first school committee session on the budget was held on Saturday, November 18, 1972.
7. The first public meeting on the Wellesley school budget was held on December 13, 1972.
8. The first budget meeting in Weston was an executive session, held on February 1, 1973.
9. Weston considered this budget estimate in December 1972. The more accurate totals were not available until February 1973. This was a two-page document giving only subtotals for each area of the school system.
10. Details from a superintendent interview in January 1973, a reported statement from the school committee meeting, *op. cit.*
11. From interviews with the superintendent, *op. cit.,* and with Mr. Ted Phillips on February 16, 1973.
12. Federal budget, fiscal year 1971.
13. Interviews with the Wellesley superintendent, January 2, 1973.
14. The assistant superintendent for personnel was well aware of the labor relations laws and, treating the QEA like a trade union, advised that a budget estimate for a contract was an "unfair labor practice." The issue is elaborated in Chapter 7.
15. This will be discussed further in Chapter 7.
16. The superintendent's main presentation was not at the session at which the school committee received the budget. It was at the meeting held two weeks later when members had acquainted themselves with the figures; on December 20, 1972.
17. *Ibid.*
18. *Ibid.,* Superintendent presentation.
19. Interview with Dr. Quin on November 17, 1973.
20. Interview with Dr. Goodman, January 2, 1973.
21. Meeting held on December 13, 1972.
22. Meeting held on February 1, 1973.
23. See Table 5-1.
24. Exchange at the school committee meeting on December 20, 1972.
25. Mr. McCauley argued against the Quincy method in the first instance at the meeting on December 6, 1972.
26. Interview with the superintendent, December 21, 1972.
27. Mr. Bud Pendleton at the public hearing on January 3, 1973.
28. Mrs. Ruth Walter, interviewed on February 14, 1973.
29. The policy had been established in the 1960s, as one of the chief tenets of the school system, when the district had an abundance of school buildings. Several internal memoranda justify the system.

30. *Ibid.*, Horace Schermerhorn's interview on February 13, 1973.

31. The superintendent was adamant to his committee and in his interview on February 8, 1973 that this was administrative, not policy work. He had even developed a policy rules book for the purpose of ensuring a clear distinction.

32. The expression was used frequently in the Quincy school committee meetings in December and January.

33. Interview with Mr. Peter Richardson, February 15, 1973.

34. This point was made by several members, but most emphatically by Chuck Crocetti on January 10, 1973.

35. Interview with Ted Phillips on February 16, 1973.

36. Interview with Robert Harvey on February 14, 1973.

37. The questions that I asked were:

> 1. Do you feel that there are any limits on the budget decisions that you can make now? (Probes) lack of free money; the economic situation and spiralling inflation, lack of sufficient information, collective bargaining, state and local regulations, public opinion and complexities of the process.
>
> 2. What changes do you feel free to make in the budget? (Probes) additions or deletions to personnel, changes to expenses, capital outlay, plant operation or instructional programs.
>
> 3. Do you feel that you can do more than change dollar allocations to items?

38. I asked them:

> 1. Do you think that the public should be more actively involved in the process of considering the budget?
>
> 2. What are the strengths and weaknesses of the present system of budget making?
>
> 3. Do you think that it is necessary to preserve all the existing programs as they are?
>
> 4. Do you think that new programs should be introduced this year?

39. Interview on February 13, 1973.

40. I asked the members:

> 1. Are you satisfied with the present system of budgeting?
>
> 2. Did the superintendent provide you with adequate information in his presentation?
>
> 3. Do you think the school committee should have its own independent staff?
>
> 4. What changes would you like to see made to the existing administrative and participant procedures?

41. The superintendent calculated this figure for the meeting on February 5, 1973.

42. The superintendent summarized the changes on January 22, 1973.

43. Interview with the superintendent on February 12, 1973.

44. The terms was first used to me by Mr. Dick Pierce in his interview on January 12, 1973.

45. These terms were used variously but especially by Dr. Robert Soule on January 10, 1973, and Daniel Raymondi on January 18, 1973.

46. Charles Sweeny on January 19, 1973.

47. Dr. Robert Soule, *op. cit.*

48. Interview with Mr. Dick Pierce, *op. cit.*

49. *Ibid.*

50. Interview with Earnest Murphy on January 5, 1973.

51. Daniel Raymondi, *op. cit.*

52. The members volunteered this phraseology. I did not ask a direct question.

53. Interview with Mary Horne, February 14, 1973.

54. Interview with Ted Phillips, *op. cit.*

55. Neal Gross, *Explorations in Role Analysis* (New York: Wiley, 1958), p. 239.

56. A short, open-ended interview is obviously not comparable with Gross' long, structured interviews. Nevertheless, none of the 26 respondents volunteered information that would fit the categories.

57. These terms were used first by the members interviewed. I asked open-ended questions. The terms were used frequently by all the members.

58. These are broad categories drawn from the interviews; the questions were open-ended.

59. The phrase was used by the superintendent in meetings and in the local newspaper, *The Patriot Ledger.*

60. Interview with Earnest Murphy, *op. cit.*

61. Interview with Robert Harvey, *op. cit.*

62. Interview with Bud Pendleton on January 5, 1973.

63. Interview with Walter Hannon, January 18, 1973.

64. Interview with David McNeish, *op. cit.*

Chapter Six

Community Involvement in Budget Deliberations

I have now discussed the interactions in the budgetary process of school committees and professional educators. They are making decisions about the educational system for the community. How do they know what the community wants and needs? In Chapter 4 I noted little actual interaction between elected representatives, as a committee or as individuals, and lay citizens over budget guidelines. Nor were there any overt communications between superintendents and the community. Are there any formal or informal mechanisms for the community, especially parents or pupils, to participate and influence budget deliberations? Is size a contributory factor? How does this affect the professional educators?

It is customary in democratic thought to consider three mechanisms for citizens to contribute to the decision process.[1] Peterson, for example, terms them democratic ritualism, the elected representatives' and interest group action.[2] Democratic ritualism refers to formal channels that representatives provide for citizen participation, but not necessarily influence. In the four districts there were two such opportunities. One was public committee meetings and the other, the public hearing. A second mechanism is more informal—interaction initiated by individual officials for voter preferences.

In the case of education, the implicit norms of behavior may be different from general, local politics.[3] There may be other informal channels, such as PTA meetings, which are not defined as budgetary process. The third mechanism is for community interest groups to initiate contact by ad hoc pressure or organized campaigns.[4] To discuss community involvement I will concentrate on use of formal machinery and informal mechanisms and from my observations of meetings and interviews. Here I base this on the operating budget, since it was the core of the budget definition.

MACHINERY FOR PUBLIC PARTICIPATION

The tradition, in most suburban communities, had been for budget meetings
to be held in executive session; they were private meetings of the committee
and professional educators. The reason was to sustain a frank debate and to
contain differences of opinion.[5] The budget has been regarded as a sensitive,
political issue.[6] The budget would normally be presented to the public both
at the beginning and end of the process, when crucial changes, if any, had been
confirmed by committee. Public presentations were a necessary but formal
convention. The committee would merely communicate its intentions publicly,
what Peterson dubs as ritualism. Tyl van Geel found a similar reason for this
method in a large city—Philadelphia:

> They (the committee) tried to keep public criticism and protest to
> a minimum but did not do so over the Athletics program.[7]

In a large district—Montgomery County—this was not how they handled debate:

> It is fair to say that public participation is regarded of great impor-
> tance to the board and school staff. It seems clear that the strategy
> of the "choices" process is to build public pressure for proposals that
> can be laid on the table to counter the requests of the Associa-
> tion.[8]

The four committees also deviated from the habitual. Quincy adopted
the most apparently distinctive form. All its meetings both for the budget
and regular business were open to the public. The meetings were announced,
and subsequently reported, in the press. Citizen attendance was invited. Indeed,
some of the budget debates were on the agenda of regular meetings. Yet they
were seen as separate from other policy issues. The public budget deliberations
were a new departure; the first at which the public was partly present was the
year before the budget for 1972.[9] The 1973-4 budget was the first entire
budget to be open to public scrutiny. Budget books were even provided for
all citizens who chose to attend.

A new member advocated open meetings because he was a former
city councillor, and his view of a public official differed from that of a regular
member of committee.[10] Since three other members were also new, he was
able, after heated debate, to convince the committee of its efficacy. Initially
a member of long standing had said:

> Some budget meetings can be pretty bloody sessions, considering
> personalities, priorities and jobs . . . . I don't think we should
> have a public brawl![11]

A new member argued that there was nothing secret about the decisions taken. The public should be allowed to attend:

> I think it is a basic right of people to know what happens to their money.[12]

In fact, the public was not able to contribute. The open meetings were not for citizen influence. Indeed, another member later commented:

> We were all on stage, playing like a bunch of actors. We had no chance to think what we were voting about. We were at a public function and not able to discuss matters.[13]

The reason was political, probably that the member wished the community to know constantly of his actions on their behalf. He therefore tried to adapt the committee's mode of operation to that of the city council, and, given no committee obstruction, did so.

The open meetings consequently were treated as a public performance. The committee viewed those in attendance as audience rather than contributors or equal participants. This matched with the notion of the superintendent as adversary: the situation became one of direct combat. There were strict rules for when and how citizens could speak to issues. Some consumer groups were given the chance to speak. The high school council was allowed four representatives to attend regularly and with all the data. The producer groups, such as teachers, were excluded from addressing certain issues. For example, the president of the local teachers' association petitioned to explain an issue during a meeting. He was refused and told to address the next meeting. He later complained that he was not given access to the budget books.[14] He was angry that the students should be, since they would not be as directly affected, nor would they be able to understand it as well. He was very conscious of the growing dissonance in the ranks of the educational profession.

In Melrose the budget meetings were also open to the public. This occured more by accident than by choice. The first budget meeting was executive, unannounced, convened quickly, and held on a Saturday morning. At it the members agreed that other budget deliberations would be held with regular meetings. Consequently, the press was present but other no other lay citizens were. The committee then moved from a regular to a budget discussion without formality. The journalist asked to follow a budget book and was casually given one, without full committee consent. The superintendent and several members reacted immediately and angrily. They did not want public disclosure of any proposed expenditures until after the whole committee had considered them. It would create too much public anxiety and, possibly, reaction to topics not yet a certainty. Several newer members argued that the public had a right to know what was being debated. They did want the journalist to be discreet about what he published. By a narrow vote, the journalist was allowed to be present, on the condition that he be cautious and tactful. The rest were open meetings available to public participation.

Little was made of the fact of public meetings. The Melrose budget were not announced separately from regular meetings. Public attendance was not specifically invited, but reports appeared in the press. As in Quincy, the public meetings did not imply participation or involvement. The formal machinery was merely made available, as in a necessary ritual. The usual mechanism of pressure group lobby was to be used for citizen participation. No special provisions were made for either teachers or pupils. Indeed, representatives of the student council did not regularly attend, but only when invited or if they had a petition. Parents were given even fewer opportunities. The superintendent stated expressly: "The PTA's are purposely not invited to budget meetings."[15] He saw the budget as a very narrow and separate activity: rather technical in content, and one in which it would be difficult for the public to make a substantive contribution.

Wellesley and Weston treated their budget meetings in the traditional suburban fashion. The superintendent proposals were presented at public committee meetings. Several closed sessions were then held before the budget was debated in public. The closed sessions were often held in collaboration with the town's financial officials. In Wellesley the reason given for closed sessions was:

> It is an opportunity for the committee to raise questions that may be embarassing to the welfare of the school system . . . . we don't want contractors to know our cost estimates for renovations . . . .[16]

In Weston the chairman favored closed meetings:

> They are so that we will not be quoted in the local paper. Reporting serves as a dampening on the free exchange of opinion![17]

The subsequent open meetings had a rigid format and schedule. At the beginning of each one, the citizens could question and present petitions. In Wellesley these were not immediately discussed but were placed on the agenda. In Weston, it was customary to answer questions in sequence. There was no other opportunity for citizens to contribute. In Wellesley, student council representatives were also included in regular committee meetings with data. In Weston, student council attendance was not a regular feature.

The Weston committee used the traditional format because of disastrous results in the previous year with a new practice. For the 1972 budget the committee had publicly debated a "smokescreen" budget in which many popular programs had been cut, at the initiative of the chairman. During debate the superintendent and committee came under much fire. The superintendent did not want a repeat performance; his reputation had suffered most.[18] He had *not* initiated many changes and yet had been forced to defend an inappropriate strategy. He successfully pressed the committee to be invisible. One member later commented that:

> ... the process was a farce. I felt really uncomfortable—it was stage-managed and the dress rehearsal was the meeting with the finance committee ... .[19]

In Wellesley and Weston there were fewer opportunities in that fewer open meetings were held. But those that were open were treated rather differently between the two towns and, even in Melrose, from those in Quincy. The members in these three did not act as at a public performance. They discussed matters more casually, but they still only allowed invited public input.

ACTUAL PUBLIC CONTRIBUTIONS

In Quincy the public made little use of the opportunity afforded them. Although there were at least 30 people present at every meeting, none of them ever spoke. There was a semblance of publicity because the room was usually packed to capacity. In fact, most of the audience were administrators and teachers. About 15 administrators regularly attended, urged by the superintendent, for support on educational matters.[20] The local press also attended regularly and fully reported the evening's events. But in the 12 meetings held, there were only about three contributions from citizens other than those on the committee. Two were from students regarding the newsheet publication. One was a reply from administrators over deferment of school supplies. No single citizen or PTA made a presentation. The one petition—on the state lunch program—was presented by a committee member. It was successful; the committee felt compelled to respond to such pressure. The meetings were, in a very real sense, a public performance and not a debate. This paralleled the previous adversary committee behavior toward the superintendent.

In Melrose, too, little use was made of public meetings. In fact, few citizens or interest groups were regularly present. Some interest groups did attend one meeting at the behest of the superintendent, because of their petitions. One elementary PTA wanted renovations to their school. The high school student council wanted an activities fund to be administered by their principal. These requests were evaluated by committee questions. The result was that the committee included them in the budget.

Another Melrose interest group did act in the process. It was formed as a result of committee action. The committee decided at its first meeting to abolish the rifle program from the athletic curriculum. The unanimous decision was to take immediate effect. As soon as it was made public, the existing rifle team formed a pressure group and campaigned to continue. It succeeded in obtaining support from many ex-servicemen and civic groups. It therefore tried to attend every subsequent meeting to present its case. By the third, a petition with 600 signatures had been collected, and the committee, noting mounting pressure, agreed to hear it. The members decided on a second vote; but, by a small majority, refused to reinstate the program. The rifle group, unabashed, continued pressure. Finally, shortly after budget ratification, a third committee vote was taken. This time the committee acknowledged the efficacy of the case, at least for the rest of the academic year. It reinstated the program, but did not guarantee its permanency. Although Melrose citizens did not make much use of formal opportunities, when they did so it was with some effect. The committee felt obliged to respond to pressure, fearing further public outrage if it did not. But it did doubt that it was responding to the majority of community opinion. In this case, it acknowledged that it had taken precipitate, if principled, action and did not want to appear to be unresponsive to some expression of community feeling.

In Weston, also, little use was made of formal channels. The previous year there had been considerable public involvement; the committee was deliberately avoiding it. No contributions were invited or made at the first two open meetings. Neither did interest groups regularly attend these meetings. At the third, the committee announced its intention to change high school foreign language offerings. In particular, it had decided to drop one, Latin, and to phase out another, Russian. This was duly reported in the local press. Thus the committee precipitated community involvement. It aroused an immediate response from those affected. Two actions resulted. The parents wrote personal and individual letters to members and the press, and parents also attended the next meeting. About 50 showed up; the meeting had to be transferred to a larger room. The committee altered its regular format and extended the time for citizens' requests.

As a result of the dialogue, the Weston committee agreed to reconsider its decision. After consultation with the superintendent and analysis by the professional educators, the committee voted to retain the program for the next session. The intention was still to phase out the programs eventually, if the pupil-teacher ratio remained low. The saving had been estimated at only 0.4 percent of the expense budget over 1972.[21] The Weston committee was willing to concede to pressure from the citizens about their needs or wishes and desires. There were not many exerted. It did not actively solicit any opinions but, in this case, had predicted some consumer reaction.

All three committees, although avoiding intense public participation, did obtain some reactions. Given their nature and volume, each committee felt compelled to respond. Their response was always to accept the fact of public interest and to handle it as if it were comprehensive. They did not, in fact, believe that the whole community had expressed its opinions, but they felt they had to respond because they saw it as their duty to allay confrontation.[22] As Lipset also demonstrates, the contributions were not in the direction of change but in maintaining the status quo.[23] The committees had not deliberately sought this out. However representative it was of the general public, it was the members' duty to be sympathetic. For example, they retained or implemented programs such as the state lunch even though the situation called for stringency. Most members did not think they should hold referenda to get majority opinions but that they should reply when citizens became vocal. The system was formally and potentially open to content changes. Summerfield also shows that school committees are "defensively wary of the vanguard which always appears just as a minority."[24]

The Wellesley committee, probably by force of circumstance, interacted more with the public than did the others. The superintendent's recommendations did not meet with the immediate approval of either the school committee or the town's advisory committee. In fact, the superintendent had not expected advisory committee approval and had predicted that he was "in for a battle."[25] Both open and closed sessions had to be used on the budget. At the first executive session, the members decided to present the public with the policy problems of the neighborhood elementary schools. The aim was to effect savings in the budget. One member initiated this move partly because she was about to retire, and also because she was encouraged by public pronouncements of local figures, most especially a former school committee member. As a selectman, he had advocated the closure of a school.[26] Indirect as well as direct pressure was of significance to Wellesley's deliberations. The school committee could not be oblivious to community demands.

The problematic issues were the location and use of elementary schools, single session kindergartens, and the implementation of the state lunch program. All hinged on the neighborhood policy. At the first open meeting, the committee announced its intentions with these issues. This was reported in the local paper. The reaction of those affected, particularly the PTA's, was instant and strong. Petitions and campaigns were organized in support of, or in opposition to, each policy. Street rallies and meetings were held; letters were sent to the press; individuals attended committee meetings.

For the next three meetings the "citizen speak" sessions were extended so that each PTA or individual parent could present a case. At each session about 15 to 20 citizens spoke. But each addressed an idiosyncratic issue: the effect of a change on his child or a particular school. No one group or individual addressed all the issues systematically. After these sessions, the public hearing, the press correspondence, and informal discussions, the committee felt that it had a sense of the prevailing mood or the town. It was to keep the status quo as regards use of elementary school buildings and kindergarten sessions but to implement the lunch program. Again, as Lipset notes, the main pressure from the citizens was towards the status quo.[27] The committee was quick to recognize this, and it wanted to be defensive.

During the sessions not only were parents involved but students as well. The senior administrators were asked to present their points of view, and two kindergarten teachers also gave a report on their schools. Principals of two elementary schools, for example, presented feasibility studies of the lunch program, which they had piloted, and its effects on teacher morale.

Apart from predicted reactions to these issues, the Wellesley public was not dissimilar to the other three, because of the committee's behavior. It did not ask for contributions from other parents, teachers, or students.

REASONS FOR USES OF FORMAL MECHANISMS

In three of the four districts there were formal opportunities for citizens, but the committees did not make them more inviting than the mere fact. They were indeed democratic rituals. The community did not make extensive use of them. Their contributions were spasmodic and intermittent, not systematic and sustained; and they came from the citizens who were, or were likely to be disaffected. They were not advice but reactions to a change of state. They did require more spending, as was the case with the rifle program or high school languages.

In the fourth district—Wellesley—the mechanisms were available and used by lay citizens, and to good effect. Size cannot be the explanation for the differences in citizen reactions. Weston's reactions compared better with Melrose than with Wellesley. The results are not apparently an effect of size but the way professional educators and school committees work for the public. First, the superintendents expected quiescence and did not anticipate community participation. They planned on amenable budget recommendations which would only require instant acceptance by the school committees. Wellesley was not a community that had a regular consensus in its school committee or between municipal officials. It was difficult for the superintendent to please the whole community with his budget, either its size or components. More participation thus occured in Wellesley than in the other areas.

The substance of citizen inputs varied, whatever the extent. In Wellesley and Weston the main inputs were around the instructional programs. In Quincy and Melrose they were more peripheral matters, such as the rifle program and 18-month budget. But both Wellesley and Quincy were unique within the state for also resisting the federally aided lunch program. These differences may have to do either with the size, wealth of community, or the priorities in that year. Since size does not explain the extent or volume of debate, it is hardly likely to account for substance. Indeed, for size to be adequate, similar evidence from Melrose is necessary. The two districts with the same government machinery were also chosen for their similar pupil costs. It is likely that the two communities openly discussed aspects of instruction because they related to what the communities could afford—educational frills or amenities.[28] Quincy and Melrose had more difficulty in sustaining an adequate core instructional program. The two towns could afford an elaborate system. Second, the Wellesley and Weston superintendents were less directive of their committees' focus away from instruction. The superintendents' roles are important even to the nature of citizen participation. Nevertheless, the differences in content were only marginal. They were not critical to the workings of the educational system. The form of citizen behavior, as reaction and not initiation, is more important to the analysis. It is clearer over other forms of citizen interaction.

THE PUBLIC HEARING

The second mechanism, another aspect of democratic ritualism, that the committees use is the public hearing. 1973 was the first year of its use throughout the state. The law stated:

> The school committee of each city, town or regional school district shall hold a public hearing on its proposed annual budget not less than 7 days after publication of a notice thereof in a newspaper, having general circulation in such city town or district. At the time and place so advertised or at any time or place to which such meeting may from time to time, be adjourned all interested persons shall be given an opportunity to be heard for or against the whole or any part of the proposed budgets.[29]

Previously school committees and municipal officials had their own machinery for budget presentation to the public. Quincy and Melrose, being cities, had both held open meetings, with scrutiny by municipal officials. Wellesley and Weston, because of their town statutes, had been obliged to present their budgets at a public hearing prior to the town meeting.

Therefore, use of the new mechanism varied. Three treated it as a formality—a way of telling the community about their intentions. The hearing was held at a point in the process so that public contributions could not have been anticipated, expected, or desired. It was used both as a way of preventing or allaying public outrage at the decisions, and also to give vital information on changes. Tyl van Geel found a similar attitude in two large school districts:

> Budget hearings . . . scheduled to permit public comment on the proposed operating and capital budget of the school system but participation in the process was not widespread because little time came between its disclosure and its final adoption by the school board.[30]

The committees in Quincy and Melrose debated whether to hold a public hearing since all their meetings had been open. They eventually recognized their legal obligations, but at a stage so late that they had to rush to it. They both only gave the minimum statutory notice in the press—seven days. Melrose did make a conscious effort to prepare for the hearing by devising an abbreviated budget book with a set of written explanations. Quincy did not prepare a written statement but at the hearing gave summaries of the main budget categories, comparisons with other cities, and a historical trend analysis. In both districts the same formula was used. The basic point was that the increase in the tax rate due to educational expenditure was levelling off. The main cause of the remaining increase lay in salary settlements and the necessary but recurrent items such as plant operation which could not easily be controlled by the school administration alone.

Size is not the factor in differences over the public hearing. Weston had a similar approach. Since the committee could not recall any extensive participation in the town's regular public hearing—and the schools constitute over two-thirds of the total budget—the superintendent advised only one public hearing.[31] This was accepted, and the town hearing was used as the school's public hearing. It was held *after* the school committee had formally approved its budget but a week before the annual town meeting.

The Wellesley committee tackled the new hearing distinctively. It held its own public hearing during deliberations, two weeks before it reached any final decisions. Indeed, two more open meetings and three executive sessions were held before the vote on the budget. The hearing was treated differently. First the budget proposals and comparative analysis of towns of similar size and wealth was presented for questions. Since there were few, various interest groups aired their grievances over the proposed policy changes. The actual hearing was very long, and the PTA's argued with each other, the members, and administrators. The crux of the debate was the proper running and administration of the school system. Both the associate superintendent and the superintendent came under heavy attack. The public hearing did engage the public for the reasons that the citizens wanted to collaborate in running the system and they were dissatisfied with the character of the programs and their administration.

DIFFERENCES IN PUBLIC HEARINGS

Participation in the hearings inevitably varied, both because of formal machinery and substance of the issues raised. The contributions in all districts illustrated some citizens' views about the running of the system. In Quincy and Melrose the statements related, on the average, to dissatisfactions with administration, and there were even personal attacks on each superintendent. In Wellesley the questions were over frustrations with existing programs as well as the specific policy raised. It was only in Weston that the citizens' questions were for clarification of matters such as salary payments.

Size again cannot be used to explain the differences between the four communities. For example, the number of questions asked was small in three communities. In Quincy only seven questions were asked; in Melrose about ten people posed about 30 questions which were interrelated; and in Weston only two questions were asked. The questions were not treated by the school committees as if they had any substance or foundation. In both Quincy and Melrose the questions related to the general direction of the system. In Weston salary was also addressed.

In any event, and more important than sheer numbers, none of the questions had any effect upon the final budgets. The questions were regarded as if they had been raised for clarification. Indeed, the superintendent in Melrose referred to many of those 50 in attendance as "cranks and paranoics."[32] The approximately 50 people in attendance at Quincy and the 100 at Weston were equally ignored, for the most part, at that point in time. The public hearing was apparently not to obtain input but rather to inform the public. Citizens probably could not make a great impact upon the budget because the tone had already been set by earlier decisions. Moreover, there were few areas of recurrent dispute that were susceptible to immediate change. Those areas requiring change were more fundamental than could be treated in one public discussion of a few hours.

The Wellesley public hearing had a different effect because it was used differently. First, almost 200 people attended, many of whom were angry about the committee's methods. They made positive recommendations stridently. At least 30 people spoke, presenting surveys and petitions on the neighborhood policy. The rest of the system, except for the activities of the administrators, was ignored. The budget itself was not given the slightest consideration. The policy issues were vehemently argued, not in cost but educational and administrative desirability.

The school committee's reaction was probably inevitable: it was to respond to pressure.[33] It was not easy to aggregate, referring to personal and idiosyncratic problems. But the pressure did point in one direction: that those affected did not want any changes in the status quo which would possibly prejudice the education of their children. The citizens did not, apparently, consider that the potential changes could lead to an improvement of the school system. The committee decided, because they believed the citizens had stated their views "loud and clear," to continue their existing policies.[34] They chose a defensive stance, in the face of all the opposition they had encountered. And yet it was from a very narrow segment of the community—some parents of pupils in a few of the eight elementary schools. Only 42 of the 240 town meeting members were present at the hearing.

The actual town public hearing in Wellesley that paralleled that in

Weston was the same as Weston's. The schools are only about half the total budget.[35] It got less than its proportional attention even though the meeting was well attended. Only one question was raised which related to the high school bond issue. The community at large may be termed apathetic, as in the other communities. Indeed, the chairman of the school committee later claims that it was.[36]

Differences between Wellesley and the others cannot be over size. Weston was more similar to both Melrose and Quincy than Wellesley. What seems to be the major factor is the superintendent's directive, which is based on the nature of the community and the predicted committee attitudes to public participation. Is this conclusion true for all types of interaction?

INDIVIDUAL MEMBERS' COMMUNICATIONS

There are two other types of communication, that between individual members and citizens. The first is initiated by members for voter preferences and the second initiated by citizens—interest group pressure.[37] Only two members interviewed—one in Quincy and one in Weston—admitted to soliciting opinions from community groups.[38] It would not produce a representative cross-section of views, which is what they hoped to achieve in their individual assessments of political mood. As the Melrose chairman put it:

> I have not felt it appropriate for members to seek out rump opinions. There are always disgruntled people in any organization . . . . [40]

However, members did get general attitudes by informal social contacts and with friends and neighbors. Most of the 26 members saw the electoral process as the main mechanism for determining local opinions. They were averse to other campaigns. They viewed the role of a public servant in terms of an individual, moral responsibility. One member actually said:

> I take a flexible approach and I'm not so much an ideologist. I shock people by taking different stands. I don't think the function of a school committee man is to go out and sound out opinion. I like people to know about me and call if they have a problem.[41]

A second member of the same committee was more emphatic: "I have stood alone. I don't want to curry favor. I am not a toady!"[42]

Nevertheless, members did not hold uniform conceptions of their duty . Many members had stood on platforms whereby they had obtained the unofficial support of political groups. Yet they did not take orders or directives but acted on the basis of individual conscience. A member in Quincy said: "The function of a school committee member is to reconcile the differences between all interest groups in the community . . . .[43] And in Weston a similar view was presented: "My job is to help manage the system to accommodate all points of view. By moving with all deliberate speed . . . .[44]

Although no member subscribed to the view that he should represent or solicit individual opinions, many mentioned contacts with some local citizens about the running of the school system. This was sufficient to know voter preference. Telephone calls and personal letters were frequently cited as the channels through which lay citizens pressed their views. Most members admitted some communications over the budget, but this did not occur often enough; they were constantly disappointed with public apathy and lack of feedback on their stands.

The members saw their role as an individual public servant, and not as part of a community. Thus no interactions or campaigns were mounted to obtain community views. The superintendent and members, by virtue of residence and/or work in the community, knew the needs without having to sound them out. In any event, aggregation of opinions or assurance of its comprehensiveness to them would have been impossible. There was no difference in this between members with a fiscally responsible attitude and those with educational interests. Styles of behavior with the superintendent did not extend to the community.

CITIZEN CONTACT WITH COMMITTEE MEMBERS

Citizens initiating interaction with the school committee is the other form of involvement. Some citizens did speak to committee members on issues that became matters of open debate. There may have been others which members did not consider worthy of committee attention, but, when interviewed, they did not cite any. Individual members did raise some issues in committee that had been brought to their attention and required action. In Quincy one new member sounded out opinion and also got citizen demands. Once he asked for improvements to tennis courts at an elementary school as a result of a teacher's request.[45] This was channelled through the superintendent and written into the budget. It passed through committee without notice or question. Similarly, citizens did exert pressure on individual members over the state lunch program. The League of Women Voters worked through one member to present a petition to the committee. A parent group was formed to press for renovations to the North Quincy High School through members and administrators. They were successful in getting a budget commitment. Yet the superintendent was concerned about the parents' protest. He felt that it was merely reactionary, a reaction to a situation, and was afraid that the parental group would not endure after completion of the issue.[46] He wanted to sustain parental involvement and was willing to respond to pressure because it indicated interest.

In Melrose citizens pressed demands through individual members rather than the committee. Members often mentioned that a citizen had pressed a point. The evaluations of athletics—such as rifle and cross country ski programs—were an outcome of pressure on the chairman of athletics. They were not of his choosing although he did express a preference during debate. The building renovations were also chosen not because of systematic evaluation but because of pressure from parent groups. A portable classroom at an elementary school, a major topic in deliberations, was initiated by the PTA with a member and the superintendent. There was also pressure from a PTA on the superintendent for better supplies for a school:

> The parents are Roosevelt are very vigorous in arguing for supplies. They even went so far as to give a party for me. So I think we should give in to them.[47]

In Weston no member brought to the committee's attention issues that had been raised individually. The chairman did mention parental pressure for better winter track facilities.[48] He expressed the belief that, on the whole, citizen pressure was over personal incidents regarding individual children. It was not a proper topic for committee.

In Wellesley instances of individual or group pressure on members are manifold. Certainly demands on individual members particularly for the state lunch program and the retention of the neighborhood policy, helped convince the committee.[49]

There was a flow of information between the committee and the public, and citizens did attempt to contribute to the educational process. But the issues raised were not fundamental. They were personal concerns or harassment: because of their informal character they are difficult to ascertain. They do not appear to be the major mechanism by which decisions are made; they are not the key to the operation of the system; but they may be critical to committee determination of policies. Yet the committees use their intuitive methods of aggregation.

COMMITTEE ATTITUDES TOWARD PARTICIPATION

Members expressed satisfaction with the defined and actual budgetary process. It was not their duty to involve the public actively by organizing meetings or soliciting opinions. They had been elected to serve as "the voice of the people," either the whole community or specific groups. Although all members, even in Wellesley, did express concern about the amount of public participation, there were no complaints about the mechanisms of budget review. Wellesley members, for example, felt that community reactions had not been very extensive and basically insufficient for policy formation. In particular, they complained about segmented involvements.

Few members had positive suggestions for changing the machinery. Indeed, the majority view was that existing mechanisms were adequate, even overgenerous. The public hearing, for instance, was possibly superfluous: its only purpose to allow members to "grandstand" to the public.[50] Only a minority had invented possible improvements in communication such as a telephone information system or annual school reviews considered naive by the others.[51]

Members did not criticize the machinery. Obviously they accepted its merits since they had stood and been elected. Second, they regarded the public as apathetic and lacking genuine interest in running the schools. Third, they felt that, most particularly regarding the budget, it was not easy for the public to express useful opinions because of the complexity of the issues.

The first reason for the acceptance of the existing system requires little explanation. The members, although having divergent community interests, had a basic belief in the democratic form of the system. They accepted the legitimacy of nonpartisan school politics and individual or personal responsibility. They also had an empirical judgment of its operations through their own election and work. It was not a sine qua non that by running for office they would be elected. Gaining office could not be treated lightly. The conventional rules of the game almost inevitably had to be accepted.

The second reason for acceptance is more complex. The notion of apathy was based on some empirical evidence. In several communities public communcation had been tried and failed. Evidence has been cited of public interest in the budget when citizens are personally affected. Apathy may not be through lack of interest but worthy issues. Given the relatively short time span of the study, an issue might not have surfaced. Nevertheless members did not know how to summon interest by means other than those tried. Moreover, this was not a priority. They had a particular conception of political representation based upon apathy. Public participation would have made their task more complicated and something of a nuisance. As one member said:

> It is almost impossible to have more participation . . . . it is difficult enough for town meeting members . . . and a frightful waste of time . . . . the public should rely on the school committee . . . .[52]

Another on the same committee was more sympathetic to the public but equally fatalistic:[53]

> People are taught that they are not supposed to understand the budget but they are starting to . . . so we're not let off lightly.[53]

Genuine citizen participation would have meant more meetings. The members did not necessarily want this since they lacked adequate free time. Apathy was also something of a rationalization for their own inability to be more involved.

Apathy was also used as a particular rationale for budget deliberations. The budget was regarded as technical and complicated and out of the realm where the public could meaningfully contribute to it. Although all members were satisfied with the system and their contribution, they stressed publicly few areas of potential change, the most important being salary. The public hearing, for example, was used to give information. The budget chairman in Melrose was the most direct:

> The budget is difficult to understand, believe me. It took me a long time. I still can't answer all the questions. I can't know everything . . . . Believe me to change anything is hard. It is impossible to fill you in on the whole process and show you everything.[54]

The members did not see the necessity of more detailed public information. They stressed the *esoteric* nature of budgeting.

SUMMARY

Lay citizens did provide some input to the budgetary process but only as the mechanisms would allow. Moreover, it was pressure, partial and personal, and therefore treated with some disdain. It was not solicited; citizens had to make some effort to contribute. There were few mechanisms—only open meetings and the public hearing. Nothing related specifically to interest groups. Apathy or rather lack of participation may be explained in ways other than through the members. First, the citizens may also be satisfied with the system, as are the members. They may have no criticisms of the system that they must articulate. Even if they are dissatisfied, the machinery available for complaints may not be very useful or effective. Citizens probably accept the form of the system as the members do. They, too, acknowledge the necessity for a social division of labor; that is, professionals running the system and elected representatives acting as guardians. The main reasons for lack of evidence of participation are probably that citizens do not believe they should contribute to the daily workings of the system. They, too, should only intervene if the system appears not to be working adequately. The citizens are not to direct the system. If this is the case, substantial participation could not be expected during the budgetary process. The budget is an example in the four districts of the continuation of the system rather than its fundamental change.

There are two corollaries to the acceptance of a social division of labor. The citizens, more than the members, might resent the time that involvement in the political process would imply.[55] Apathy is not necessarily the reason for the apparent indifference. It is more likely to be conformity to the prevailing norms that makes time necessary for adequate citizen input. The issues are complex, yet lack of participation also does not necessarily mean acknowledgement of the need for professional expertise; that is, educational knowledge to run the budget. It is probably that involvement in the system requires basic knowledge of local conditions and budgeting. Both are not easy to acquire. Citizens are not brought up to believe that they are capable or should help make decisions on their own community. The citizens agree with their representatives.

Size does not appear to be crucial to amount of community involvement in the budgetary process. General lack of participation is a result of the rules of the game which are well taught throughout society. Neither the adversary and the ally style of committee behavior produces more involvement. Both result in public displays rather than collaboration. These styles affect only process and not outcome. The division of labor remains essentially the same— the professional educators are in ascendance. It is the superintendent's preferences which condition the budget. Changes occur at the margins because of individual idiosyncracies, but they are not a regular and systematic occurrence. The system is not organized to allow for constant collaboration. Indeed, in these budget deliberations there were few areas worthy of note. Nevertheless, professional educators have to be constantly aware of potential action by the citizens and likely interactions with their school committees. If they do not succeed, conflict may break out. Their attention over the budget, however, has to be given not to the lay community but to its representatives as municipal officials.

NOTES TO CHAPTER SIX

1. See, for example, Robert A. Dahl, *Who Governs?* (New Haven: Yale University Press, 1963), p. 34.
2. Paul Peterson and Paul Kantor, *Partisanship and the Limits of Democratic Theory* (Unpublished paper, University of Chicago, 1970), p. 11
3. See, for example, Michael Kirst (ed.), *The Politics of Education at the Local, State and Federal Levels* (Berkeley: McCutchan, 1970).
4. See, for example, M. Kirst and F. Wirt, *The Political Web of American Schools* (Boston: Little Brown, 1972).
5. M. Kirst, *op. cit.,* introduction.
6. *Ibid.;* see also ch. 3.
7. Tyl van Geel, *Efficiency, Effectiveness and Local School Systems* (Unpublished doctoral dissertation, Harvard Graduate School of Education, 1972), p. 188.
8. *Ibid.,* p. 223.
9. Report in *The Patriot Ledger,* January 13, 1973.
10. Interview with Francis X. McCauley, January 17, 1973.

11. Francis Anselmo, reported in *The Patriot Ledger,* January 13, 1973.
12. Francis McCauley, *op. cit.*
13. Anselmo, reported in *The Patriot Ledger, op. cit.*
14. Interview with Mr. Harold Crowley, Chairman of Q.E.A., January 25, 1973.
15. Interview with Dr. Quin, January 12, 1973.
16. Interview with Dr. Goodman, January 2, 1973.
17. Interview with Mr. Ted Phillips, February 16, 1973.
18. Interview with Dr. Wood, December 19, 1972.
19. Interview with Joan Wexler, February 19, 1973.
20. Interview with Dr. Creedon, *op. cit.,* and discussions at the LMT and IPT meetings, November 1972.
21. See Weston's internal budget documents for 1973–74.
22. Interviews with 26 school committee members January–February 1973. I asked them, "What do you think your task as a school committee member is?"
23. S.M. Lipset, In C.A. Bowers et al. (eds.), *Education and Social Policy* (New York: Random House, 1970), p. 34.
24. Harry Summerfield, *The Neighborhood-based Politics of Education* (Columbus Ohio: Merrill, 1971), p. 101.
25. Interview with Dr. Goodman, November 28, 1972.
26. Interview with Ruth Walter, February 14, 1973, and David Sargent's speech reported in the *Townsman,* December 29, 1972.
27. Lipset, *op. cit.,* pp. 34, 37.
28. Summerfield, *op. cit.,* makes similar points. In a review in the *Harvard Educational Review* he is taken to task for the brevity of the study. See Jeffrey Raffel, *HER* (February 1972).
29. Chapter 649, Public Laws 1972 section 38N.
30. Tyl van Geel, *op. cit.,* p. 84.
31. Interview with Dr. Wood, *op. cit.*
32. Telephone conversation with Dr. Quin, January 4, 1973.
33. Compare Summerfield's conclusions, *op. cit.*
34. Interview with David McNeish, *op. cit.*
35. The tax rate for 1972 was $48; that for schools, $26.
36. Interview with David McNeish, *op. cit.*
37. Peterson, *op. cit.*
38. Interviews with Joan Wexler of Weston and Harold Davis of Quincy.
39. I asked the members:
    "Have you talked to the public—parents, community groups or associations—prior to making your decisions?
    Did they press for talks or did you request them?
    Do you think that you should sound out opinion prior to receiving the tentative budget?"
40. Interview with Dr. Robert Soule, January 10, 1973.
41. Interview with Earnest Murphy, January 5, 1973.
42. Interview with John Couglan, January 11, 1973.
43. Interview with Harold Davis, January 18, 1973.

44. Interview with Ted Phillips, *op. cit.*
45. The teacher who in fact made the request was a sister of the committee member!
46. Interview with Dr. Creedon, *op. cit.*
47. Comment at an internal meeting, November 3, 1972.
48. Interview with Ted Phillips, *op. cit.*
49. Letter from Mrs. Jean Kelly, June 25, 1973.
50. John Couglan, *op. cit.*
51. Interviews with Joan Wexler, February 19, 1973, and Harold Davis, *op. cit.*
52. Interview with Bob Harvey, February 14, 1973.
53. Jean Kelly, *op. cit.*
54. Mr. Bud Pendleton, at the public hearing, *op. cit.*
55. R.A. Dahl, *op. cit.,* p. 306.

Chapter Seven

Salary Negotiations

In previous chapters I explored the development of the operating budget. I have shown the critical role which professional educators play in it. The analysis has touched on all aspects of budgeting—including deciding upon personnel numbers and types—except that of salaries. Yet the educational process is labor-intensive, which is to say that one of its main resources is personnel. Indeed, approximately 80 percent of the annual budget is appropriated to salaries, as Table 2-6 has shown. Moreover, about 80 percent of each salary bill goes to the professional employees—teachers and administrators. Table 7-1 compares the districts. Do the same relationships hold between the various participants in the process of deciding on contracts, salary scales, and increases? Are the professional educators critically influential and, if not, what is the nature of influence in this? Is size a mediating factor in the influences? This chapter seeks to answer these questions and to define the professional educators' sphere of influence. It focuses only on salaries for professional educators since they are the bulk of the staff, and concern is with professional control.

Given the organization of the educational system, one may presume citizen control over the salary decisions. As with other educational decisions, school committees have full responsibility to determine terms of contract,

Table 7-1. Salary for Professional Employees, 1971-2

	Professional Salaries as a Percent of Total
Quincy	83
Melrose	79
Wellesley	75
Weston	75

Source: Data from superintendent proposals and presentations, January–February 1973.

salary scales, and annual salary increases.[1] There are no official rules imposed by state or federal governments. Machinery on labor relations does vary between states, although it does not change the locus of control.[2] It regulates the type of possible negotiations. Guidelines may be enunciated by the federal government for resource allocation in the national interest. Indeed, wage and price restraints to control inflation have been imposed by the federal government since 1970.[3] The government does not pronounce on maxima or minima for salary scales.[4] Ostensibly school committees control these decisions. (This is in direct contrast, for example, to Britain. There, negotiations take place at the level of national government for both professional and non-professional staff.)

Representative or lay control seems inevitable. If the process is open to public scrutiny, citizens may pronounce on decisions with variations according to government machinery.

Also, fiscal autonomy is a very weak concept for salary negotiations in Massachusetts because of practical developments. Salary scales for the professional educators are set for the academic year, whereas the operating budget has traditionally been set for the calendar year. Since the actual timing of the two processes is not synonymous, two salary contracts usually have to be included in the annual operating budget. For school committees to have fiscal autonomy by statute, decisions have to be fully ratified by April 1st of the budget year. In actuality, school committees are not always able to complete salary negotiations by this date and settle the next contract since they cannot predict with accuracy their salary bill. There are two possible strategies available, each of which has different controls over personnel. One is to estimate the likely amount and budget it. Alternatively, the committee may await the conclusion of negotiations in the belief that to put an estimate in the budget is an "unfair labor practice," that is, prejudicial to negotiations.[5] If the salary bill is not approved within the budget, school committees relinquish their fiscal autonomy. They have to apply to the municipal officials for special approval for the salary settlement. Given this, there is a real possibility of citizen influence over outcome, if not process. There is evidence from the studies of large cities that the mayor has acted as an official mediator in negotiations.[6]

Size of district may affect process in that it concerns the relations between participants. In this case, the smaller the district the greater the likelihood of an interchange between the school committee and its employees. In smaller districts the professional bureaucracy should be smaller and possibly less well organized than a larger into a hierarchical system. The professional employees will not necessarily have the administrative and organizational resources to influence decisions as in the larger districts. Gittell, for example, showed how the main source of influence in a large city school system was the professional bureaucracy—administrators—and not the superintendent or the teachers.[7]

MACHINERY FOR SALARY NEGOTIATIONS

The process of deciding on teachers' salary scales and contracts is now generally separate from the operating budget. This is not only because of scheduling but also the changing concept of labor relations in the USA.[8] Originally salary settlements were an intrinsic part of the budgetary process because suburban school systems were run like a family business.[9] Teachers and administrators did not see themselves as "workers"; settlements were reached by gentlemanly agreement. Kirst and Wirt described the situation:

> For many years the most numerous interest group—the teachers—
> had only potential political power. Traditionally schoolteachers
> have been reluctant to employ collective action to transmit demands
> to political authorities either within or outside of the school system.
> Further, the doctrine of school administrators played down the
> usefulness of collective organization of tea hers, stressing instead
> the use of negotiations by individual professionals.[10]

The superintendent, acting on behalf of his professional staff, that is, the teachers and administrators, would reach agreement with his school committee. As Kirst and Wirt state further, "The traditional doctrine was that each teacher should negotiate with the superintendent." Actual scales and levels of increase were reached on market principles; the superintendents would not only consider comparable occupations and locally available resources but would also try to compete with neighbouring and districts of similar wealth. The purpose of competitive salary scales was to attract the best teachers to the school district, assuming that salary was the main criterion of occupational and geographical choice.

In the 1950s and 1960s teachers began to see the problems and iniquities in this system, and they grouped themselves collectively.[12] Two separate organizations developed. In the large cities the American Federation of Teachers (AFT) gained currency and increased its membership. It restricted its entry strictly to rank and file teachers, and not to administrators who had supervisory positions over teachers.[13] Its avowed purpose was to win better conditions of employment for teachers, both by acting as a general pressure group and through negotiations with employers. However, as Koerner states:[14]

> The great majority of classroom teachers belong to their local and
> state NEA, but only a shade over half of them belong to the national
> body.

The NEA—the National Educational Association—had as its purpose the campaigning for a unified profession, and at the federal and state levels it acted as a pressure group for educational interests. It included in its membership superintendents and administrators. But, at the same time, the local associations began to recruit members with the express purpose of changing their working conditions. They also began to press for salary negotiations with local employers.

As a result of pressure in the 1960s, the State of Massachusetts changed its labor relations laws. Not every state responded thus. In 1965 the state legalized collective bargaining between employers and their employees.[15] It restricted bargaining by specifying only one official unit for each set of employees.[16] For the teachers, that is generally the Massachusetts Teachers Association (MTA) or its local affiliate. No machinery was set up for the collective action of the employers, and the local school committee remained the unit.

Thus the formal situation changed. The actual local developments were slow to occur. However, the traditional view of professional employees who would arrive at agreements with their employers was slowly eroded by the new machinery. The notions of the roles of participants were considerably altered. How has this come about in the four school districts? In what way do the professional educators now act?

ACTUAL NEGOTIATIONS

In all four school districts changes have occurred in the machinery and its use for negotiations, but these changes have not been uniform. First, the committees have adopted more formal methods of negotiations with most of the professional employees. (The superintendent and his immediate colleagues still negotiate separately and individually with their school committees.) The committees no longer rely on the superintendents to present their case to the teachers or to bring the teachers' demands to them. All the committees use a lawyer as negotiator, but the types vary. In Melrose and Weston the proceedings for the 1972–3 contract were conducted by a member of the school committee because he was a lawyer.[17] In Melrose a negotiating team of three members, all of whom were lawyers, appointed one chief negotiator. In Weston, the 1972 chairman of the committee was a labor relations lawyer for a large Boston company. His predecessors, some six years previously, had asked him to run for committee, precisely because of his expertise.[18] He conducted the negotiations in front of the other members. Quincy and Wellesley employed an expert labor relations attorney.[19] Some members, as a special negotiating team, were appointed to attend the meetings, but they did not conduct the proceedings. They had recently adopted the practice of hiring a lawyer, having relied on their own resources. The lawyer on the Quincy school committee, who five years previously had run for election to conduct negotiations, had demanded the hiring. He claimed that:

> I spent 3 to 4 nights a week. I was new to the committee and I learned a lot. . . .I had to do a lot of studying and homework . . .

but it's too much time . . . . a waste of time . . . . so I recommended that we get counsel.[20]

The Wellesley committee had also decided to hire a negotiator for the 1972-3 contract. No one member had the appropriate skills or time.

For the 1973-4 contract Weston continued to use the committee chairman. Once he retired, the committee would no longer rely on its own resources but would hire a negotiator. Having negotiated a two-year contract in 1972, the Melrose committee had no reason to negotiate in 1973. But they also considered hiring a lawyer for future negotiations.

The differences in practice between communities were not very great. Essentially they were all moving in the same direction, but at varying rates, to more business and bureaucratic methods. The use of either an internal or external lawyer is a function of the idiosyncratic characteristics of the members and not size.

There were grave consequences to these practices. The committee relations with, and uses of, the superintendent also changed, but with district differences, dependent upon superintendents' attitudes. In Quincy the superintendent did not attend the negotiations sessions, nor did he provide direct advice to the committee. He allowed an assistant superintendent to act on his behalf. The Wellesley committee used an assistant superintendent. In the two previous years, the superintendent had attended, but both he and the committee had not found it useful. In Weston, too, the main aid to the committee was the assistant and not the superintendent. Indeed, for the 1973-4 contract, at least two meetings were scheduled and held without the superintendent's knowledge.[21] In Melrose, the superintendent did attend and advise on the negotiations sessions for the 1972-3 contracts. He had developed an interest in the legal aspects of negotiations. It was only in Melrose that the superintendent had close involvement in the actual process. The other superintendents chose not to involve themselves. They did not define that as an area of their interest or one in which they could have any great effect. It was separate from school policies and did not relate to education per se.

The professional employees had also developed new procedures since 1965 and the superintendents were similarly conspicuous by their absence from the proceedings. All had professional associations which were affiliates of the Massachusetts Teachers Association. They each catered for over 80 percent of the professional employees, as Table 7-2 shows, and elected negotiating teams for bargaining. They also relied on the resources of the MTA.

For the 1972-3 contract, a nine-member team of the Quincy Educational Association (QEA) negotiated for all teachers and administrators, except for a central office team. The latter, the LMT, negotiated separately with the school committee, using the superintendent as their chief negotiator. The QEA team negotiated for the rest of the professional staff. At the end of

Table 7-2. Membership of Professional Associations, 1972

	Members	*Total Educators*
Quincy	807	950
Melrose	285	401
Wellesley	380	459
Weston	—	262

Source: Information from the teachers' representatives.

these negotiations, which were particularly harrowing and acrimonious, some other central office administrators—the Instructional Planning Team—decided to resign from membership of the QEA and seek separate negotiating machinery.[22]

A five-member team of the Melrose Educational Association (MEA) negotiated for all teachers and administrators for the 1972-3 contract. Only the superintendent and his central office staff were excluded. At the end of the sessions for 1972-3, the superintendent persuaded all the administrators to break away and set up their separate unit, although even within the MEA the administrators negotiated separate contracts.[23]

The seven-member team of the Wellesley Teachers' Association negotiated for all teachers and administrators, except for the central office staff. The team negotiated two separate contracts—one for teachers and one for administrators. Indeed, in the 1974 contract a new form of payment was introduced for the administrators, based on merit rather than seniority.[24] The teachers refused to countenance such a change in contract.

In Weston the five-member team, for the first time in 1973, negotiated for all teachers and administrators except for a central office staff. Hitherto, staff had discussed separate memoranda of agreement for each category, teacher and administrator.[25]

The marginal differences between type of professional association do appear to be related to size of system and its bureaucracy. The new division in the professional educators' ranks in Quincy and Melrose may have to do with size and ability of the various levels of staff to organize themselves. On the other hand, they may be associated with community wealth. The splits in Quincy and Melrose occurred because of the substance of negotiations—questions about salary scale and increase. Being less wealthy communities, they could not afford to pay high salaries and did not seek to be at the top of the league. The teachers pressed for this, but the administrators were not so adamant and did not want to employ the teachers' militant tactics, such as strike threats. In Weston and Wellesley disaffection between teacher and administrators was not yet apparent, perhaps because offers of salary increase were less derisory.

All the local associations did not only rely on their own resources but also used the MTA, again variably. The president of the Quincy Educational

Association was allowed a sabbatical leave to negotiate the 1973-4 contract. He only used the MTA for advice and information. The MEA also only used the MTA as a resource. In Wellesley and Weston, a full-time negotiator from the MTA acted on behalf of the teams at the conference table. The use of the MTA may have militated against splits between teacher and administrators and yet be the result of wealth and not size of community.

District differences do not appear to be very significant. The local associations are moving in the same direction toward legal and formal negotiations. None of them used the central office administration. They had little or no contact with the superintendent over negotiations. Indeed, they disdained asking for his help, not viewing him as a colleague.

The key participants in salary negotiations were the school committees, their lawyers, and employee negotiating teams, with or without state help. The superintendent and his central office staff did not play an ostensibly major role. Does this mean an actual difference in spheres of influence in this process or does the machinery belie its real nature?

CONTENT OF NEGOTIATIONS

The contents of negotiations, although over 70 percent of the budget, were narrow and specific in subject matter.[26] They were about the actual size of salary increase and the relative levels of salary scales for qualifications and experience. Although the amount of money under consideration was large, the range of discretion over the annual increase could not be great. The number of employees and their salaries were set basically from year to year. For either of the two contracts studied—1972-3 or 1973-4—national wage and price restrictions were in force to stem inflation. No salary increase offered could be greater than 5 percent. For this reason, two teacher teams—those in Melrose and Wellesley—finally settled on two-year contracts which included annual increases of almost 5 percent. To reach agreement they had to go to arbitration and also request an additional municipal appropriation.

In essence, negotiations were played within tight constraints. Few changes could be considered or implemented. The committees contemplated altering terms of employment from the traditional of a career and promotion ladder, predicated on seniority to contracts based on merit payments.[27] None of the teacher units accepted the idea. The Wellesley administrators agreed to experiment with a modified version for the 1973-4 year. They would help to develop the terms of merit evaluation.

Also part of the subject matter were matters of teachers' welfare but not the direction of the educational system per se. These matters covered types of leave and remuneration for specific skill.[28] The contracts also related to working conditions such as hours, length of school year, and teaching load. Yet the pupil-teacher ratio per se was not a matter for negotiation. The committee issued statements on class size. In the Weston contract, the one most favorable to teachers, for example, the statement was also made:

> Class size . . . . final decisions on these matters remain in the sole discretion of the school committee.[29]

All the negotiating teams raised issues affecting the direction of the school system. They had to haggle over them as a proper subject for negotiation and certainly did not achieve the demands. In Quincy, for example, some of the longest discussions over the 1972-3 contract concerned lunch duty for teachers. The team was unable to wring concessions from the school committee. In Weston the teachers tried to negotiate about academic freedom and professional representation on committees but did not make much headway.

ACTUAL ROLES IN THE PROCESS

Salary negotiations, although concerning the largest item of the budget, involved a small number of participants over a narrow range of matters. Who, then, was critically influential and over what did they have an impact? First, each school committee negotiated in private with the bargaining teams for the 1972-3 contract. The sessions were not public: control was between professional educators or school committees. Lay citizens, as such, were not given any opportunity to participate in determining contracts.

     For the 1973-4 contract one school committee decided to alter this procedure. The Quincy committee would hold open all its negotiating sessions.[30] It explicitly invited the public to attend. The other committees did not choose to do this. The Quincy committee took this strategy defensively. The same adversary style of behavior toward the superintendent was used to the teachers. The reason was an attempt to reduce teachers' influence. The advocate of the new strategy said, "I want to make the teachers realize that they look like fools to the public. I think their demands are unreasonable."[31] Indeed, although the machinery accords critical influence to the school committee, there is evidence that the members did not feel unilaterally in control.

     Other machinery was used for the community to influence negotiations, but only the outcome, not the process. It related to the setting of a salary ceiling or an estimate of the increase and not the final figure. In the cities of Quincy and Melrose the mayors could not make independent contributions. The negotiations were conducted between the teachers and school committee. There is no evidence that the mayor or the financial officials played any special part by setting guidelines such as salary ceilings or estimates. The mayor in Quincy only acted as chairman of the school committee. He was as involved as the other members in agreeing the salary changes. Yet negotiations in 1972 had gone to state abritration, and the municipal officials had appropriated an extra amount than what was in the budget.

In Melrose, the mayor made a small attempt to influence the situation but was rebuffed. In the fall of 1972 he announced publicly teacher contracts, and that he had agreed to appropriate the necessary additional sum, a result of independent arbitration. He added that if there were dissatisfied teachers, the MEA president should consult with him. The school committee and the superintendent were extremely affronted, regarding it as an infringement of their rights. The MEA president was prepared to negotiate but did not do so because of the conventional rules that negotiations take place in a closed system between schoolmen. Citizens were able to contribute at the public hearings, but in neither Quincy nor Melrose did they choose to.

In the two towns municipal officials and lay citizens played a more overt role. In Weston several meetings between the school and finance committees on the budget, in fact, solely revolved around the salary settlement.[32] The finance committee, at pains to determine the budget total, tried to force some "moral" agreement from the school committee about the increase to be offered. It was successful in that a ceiling was put on the potential salary increase and an estimate of the total new salary bill written into the budget. This figure had to be agreed upon prior to budget approval by the finance committee and the town meeting. The chairman of the school committee, who had initially been opposed to estimates on the grounds that they were not good for actual haggling, eventually concurred.[33] He later claimed that the estimate was generous and would not constrain his tactics. The estimate in the budget was one jointly arrived at by the finance and school committees. The finance committee had used its potential influence over the school committee, and with effect. No special town meeting would be necessary. The Wellesley superintendent claimed that a similar collaboration and joint determination usually took place. It did not happen in 1973 because of the two-year settlement in 1972. This had required state arbitration and a special appropriation of funds. Indeed, the other non-professional contracts were negotiated annually by the town's personnel board, an indication of agreed collaboration and citizen influence.

Weston's machinery for citizen participation was used to discuss salary. Salary was the topic of debate at the public hearing and the town meeting.[34] The chairman of the school committee raised it by separating the presentation of his negotiations from that of the operating budget. Only two questions were raised; both concerned salary. At the town meeting teacher negotiations were also pinpointed in the budget presentation, but that did not make for any public reaction. Wellesley's town meeting also provided a forum for citizen debate on teachers' salaries. In fact, no questions were asked.

In sum, each community did provide some opportunities for citizens to participate in salary settlements. In the two towns, the officials not only contributed but exerted some influence, and effectively. In the cities, municipal pronouncements indirectly affected negotiations. Government machinery may be insufficient to explain the differences in influences on process. In all, the final settlements for 1972-3 required a new appropriation. Wealth of the communities may be important. The two towns may have been more conscious of their spending because of having more choices to manipulate. The Melrose and Quincy committees recognized their limited choice.

Although both school committees and municipal officials played a part in negotiations, the evidence is not conclusive that they were critically influential. Both Quincy's new public meetings and Wellesley's merit pay contracts indicate lack of self-assurance on the part of the community's representatives. Weston's consideration of a consortium of school committees to negotiate collectively is another indication of the members' concern. The aim was to counteract the apparent incipient influence of teachers. There is, however, no evidence that all the professional educators played a key role in negotiations. Indeed, in three school districts the superintendents did not attend negotiations, nor did they have any contact with the teachers. They did not claim to help the committee reach agreement on the salary offer. Rather they called themselves resources to the school committee.[35] Were the teachers, then, the most influential participants in the process?

All the negotiations in fact, were bitter and long. In three, the teachers threatened to take action to force the committee to relent on the salary increase for 1972-3. In Quincy the teachers took off one day to hold a discussion on how to obtain their demands. In Wellesley the teachers staged a protest demonstration as had the teachers in Melrose the previous year. An outside arbitrator was called in to help settle the terms of the contract. There is evidence that the teachers were able to force certain decisions from the committees and that they did not permit the committees to impose certain contracts. They all refused, for example, to countenance merit pay.

The evidence is not very strong that any one set of participants was the chief influence over negotiations for the 1972-3 contract. Rather collective bargaining appears to have affected the division of labor to such an extent that none of the participants feel that they have decisive impact. This is obvious from the attitudes of professional educators and committee members. What is more apparent is that professional control by superintendents here is lacking because of the divisions among professional educators.

ATTITUDES TOWARD NEGOTIATIONS

All participants felt that collective bargaining had wrought changes in the division of labor and actual influence in the decision-making process. Most particularly, it had affected the role of superintendent. Previously, the superintendent had been the lynchpin, negotiating all contracts or salary terms. Now, because of the structure of the situation, the four superintendents found it necessary to change their role. Three had decided to define the negotiating situation narrowly and opt out of the part over which they could have no immediate influence. The Quincy superintendent said, "I play no part in the negotiating sessions but I do set the main parameters."[36] He therefore left details to his assistant superintendent. The Wellesley superintendent also excluded himself from the day-to-day proceedings:

> Now I am in a much better position than previously when I went to the meetings. I don't want to deal with the nitty-gritty. If I do I will lose sight of the broader picture . . . . and that's my main job.[37]

Only the Melrose superintendent attended and conducted the meetings.

These choices of tactic seem to be more a matter of individual interest and energy than of political necessity. The superintendents were free to choose and did so to maximize their own influence over the decision process. They excluded themselves, on the whole, from discussions over salary and pure finance matters but not over educational issues concerning salary settlements. They regarded themselves as resources to committee. On all other matters, they would give more definitive educational advice.

The committees used the superintendents' definitions of the situation. They agreed that the superintendents were a resource to them on purely financial issues. They still needed the superintendents' advice over working conditions, pupil-teacher ratios and educational programs.

The new machinery had affected the superintendents' role in another direction. They could no longer see themselves as representative of teachers. They now did not even attempt to profer advice to teachers over negotiations. They saw themselves strictly as executives of the school committee and the educational leader of the school system. Their role was that of manager and controller rather than part of the teaching profession. The Quincy superintendent said:

> The job of the superintendent is to be the executive of the school committee and to handle the tasks generated by them. I am not the teachers' representative or their employer. Nor do I put the school committee case. I am just the spokesman for the educational community—I stand between the committee and the teachers.[38]

The Melrose superintendent espoused rather less of a mediator position:

> I am an advisor to the school committee. Collective bargaining has changed all the relations. I used to be with the teachers. Now I am 100% an agent of management. This makes my other positions difficult for I cannot go into the schools just when I have disciplined a teacher . . . . so it is now a whole different ball game. But it's much more logical.[39]

These statements indicate that the superintendents believe they should set the educational objectives and means of achievement by the teachers. They should oversee teachers' activities. The superintendents no longer have a unity of interest with teachers. As Kirst and Wirt stated in a general vein: "Professional unity is a myth, because value conflicts are inevitable between teachers and their managers who administer the schools."[40]

The committees again accepted the superintendents' definitions. They also claimed that superintendents were not the teachers' representative. They saw him as part of the management system. Other professional educators—the central office administrators—also indicated a lack of unity with teachers. They, too, accepted that the superintendent was not the teachers' representative, not allying themselves to the teachers but also part of the management system. A junior high school principal in Melrose mentioned that:

> I am now a step removed from the teachers. I used to be the teacher spokesman. Now I'm middle management and drifting away from teacher representation . . . and moving towards the school committee.[41]

The associate superintendent in Melrose also stressed his managerial role:

> I see myself as aligned to the teachers . . . . my office is at the high school. But it is a little awkward because I am the arm of the school committee. At times I have conflicts of interest with the superintendent over enforcing contracts with the teachers.[42]

The central office administrators found, indeed, that they were often in a difficult position. This was most often true for the associate superintendents for curriculum or instruction. They were very involved in educational matters but found themselves having to be managers. They did not want to become superintendents because the role lacked much educational content: it was very managerial. They all expressed some conflicts in their own roles with teachers and superintendents.[43]

Moreover, central office administrators' tactics over their own bargaining indicate the increasing tensions within the educational profession. In particular, the Instructional Planning Team in Quincy and the coordinators and directors in Melrose asserted their independence of the teachers by creating their own bargaining teams. This indicated their expressed managerial role.

The teachers also confirmed these definitions. They did not regard the superintendent as their representative. Kirst and Wirt had presented a general view of the situation: "More often now the teachers will not let the administrators be their spokesmen for good educational policy."[44] The advent of collective bargaining had affected divisions within the educational profession. But the splits also occurred because of differences in educational focus and client systems. The president of the QEA expressed the conflict bluntly: "The superintendent's priorities are not mine. I don't profess to understand his. . . ."[45] The president of the MEA was even more emphatic:

> The superintendent is on the other side. He is the enemy in negotiations. He is not one of the faculty. The administrators are also on the other side of the fence.[46]

The Weston teachers' president held a somewhat similar view of the superintendent:

> Yes. The superintendent is an adversary. He is not a resource for the teachers. But I must admit I have never asked him for his advice. In day to day life he may be the spokesman for the schools and the teachers. But he doesn't visit the schools much. I don't see him very often . . . .[47]

This confirms the statement made by Myers: "Administrators have been shunted aside as adversaries in the process of collective bargaining."[48]

The professional educators are no longer a homogeneous occupational group but are very divided in their ranks. They do not see themselves as colleagues and allies. The superintendents and administrators are concerned with management and teachers with the process of learning. Yet the teachers do not think that this division of tasks has led them to wrestle control from the administrators over either collective bargaining or the education process. They are stil trying to change the situation. Kirst and Wirt spoke to the point:

> Teachers, repudiating the turn of the century doctrine stressing the harmony of the profession, are using collective bargaining to wring concessions from school boards and administrators.[49]

The teachers in the four districts do not feel that they have achieved much. They are still excluded from key roles in the educational decision-making process. They have not been allowed to negotiate over a wide range of issues.

The superintendents also do not feel that the teachers have taken over control. They themselves have defined the situation narrowly, and have excluded the teachers or used the method of divide and rule. The superintendents also do not accord the school committee control over salaries. The situations has been constructed so that it is very difficult for the committees to stay the power of more widely based professional associations. The teacher associations have at least a constraining effect on negotiations. Because they are able to draw support from other teacher associations, their potential influence is increasing, whereas the committees have no such body. This point became clear over certain substantive issues such as merit pay. Not only did the local teachers refuse to endorse it but also the Massachusetts Teachers' Association backed them and refused to sanction any such schemes. The state association aimed to develop a unity of purpose among teachers if not between teachers and administrators. The practice of merit pay would be inimical to such an end. It would also, in all probability, erode the strength of the teacher associations, just as the school committees proposing such an approach intended it to do.

SUMMARY

The control of negotiations is different from that of the operating budget. There is evidence of the use of machinery for representative participation and influence over the process. The committee members did not act as legitimators of the school superintendents but actually themselves negotiated the salary scales, increases, and contracts. The superintendents played a small part. However, the crucial point is that the members did not believe that they were influential. They do not feel really free to make decisions: the rules were, in fact, set elsewhere than by the committee. Neither did the teachers, to whom the committees attributed major influence, believe that they themselves can obtain satisfactory settlements.

The division of labor in the education profession has curtailed the spheres of influence of all participants. Now the rules of negotiations do not allow for professional or citizen control. There is no evidence of professional control because of the increasing divisiveness in the profession of educators. Although the superintendents are not influential over salary scales and increases, they do have influence over working conditions. The teachers have not so far succeeded in making gains in this area. What is more, it is still true that the superintendents have the choice to decide whether to take part in negotiations. They themselves defined the situation.

What emerges from the analysis is that professional control is diffuse in the area of negotiations. Collective bargaining has curtailed the amount of professional influence wielded by the superintendents rather than increased it. Although the superintendents see themselves as the professional and educational leaders of the school system, they are not automatically treated as charismatic leaders by the teachers. In fact, the teachers see conflicts of interest, thus refuting the validity of their influence. The superintendents' task is concerned with bureaucracy and administration.

Size does have some effect on the nature of professional control. The divisiveness in the profession is not yet as great in the smaller school districts—Weston and Wellesley—as in the larger. But a similar dissonance in ethos was beginning to emerge. Even Weston's teachers did not hold the same interests with the superintendent, as they did prior to the collective bargaining. It was noticeable to the extent that a school committee member remarked:

> The teachers talk to me and tell me their problems and dissatis-
> factions. They don't go to the superintendent. He is too much of
> a "Case House" administrator. He doesn't get into the schools.[50]

The conclusion is that administrative professionalism in education, although ostensibly more concerned with education matters per se, is not confined to the learning process. The emergent splits in the profession lead the superintendents to act as managers rather than as educators, and to control the teaching profession. The teachers are also gaining strength, as Rosenthal says: "Teachers are gaining more power. One basic trend is the increasing strength and vitality of teacher groups."[51] Although collective bargaining is obviously a special case of professional control at the local level, lay control is not greater in collective bargaining than it is with the operating budget. But the superintendents are no longer crucially influential. The other ranks of profession, especially since the foment in the large cities in the 1960s, are now gaining on them. Rosenthal predicts:

> In the future there is the likelihood of more extensive and perhaps
> intensive conflict accompanying a widening cleavage between
> teachers and administrators. All this will probably result in still less
> effective control by lay school boards and a whittling away of the
> discretionary authority of school administrators . . . . a formal
> framework of collective bargaining or professional negotiations
> enhances still more the power position of individual teachers and
> teacher organizations in the school system.[52]

There is no longer any harmony in the profession. The main potential strength now lies with the teacher associations. Although the superintendents as professional educators still have the discretion to control their own market situations and, therefore, the direction of educational policies, they do not control the entire profession or its main interests. Indeed, control is being wrested from them. The teachers are beginning to be influential because of their collective techniques of organization. As yet, the changes are still potential and the superintendents rely on the technique of divide and rule to maintain their position. The school committees still look to the superintendents for advice and help. But changes are emerging.

NOTES TO CHAPTER SEVEN

1. For more details see Roald Campbell, et al., *The Organization and Control of American Schools* (Columbus, Ohio: Merrill, 1970), ch. 4.

2. *Ibid.,* ch. 5.

3. See C. Schultze, et al., *Setting National Priorities: The 1971 Budget* (Washington, D.C.: Brookings, 1970), p. 9.

4. Michael Kirst (ed.), *The Politics of Education at the Local, State and Federal Levels* (Berkeley: McCutchan, 1970), part 3.

5. This point was made emphatically by the assistant superintendent for personnel in Quincy in an interview on December 21, 1972.

6. Kirst, *op. cit.;* M. Gittell and T.E. Hollander, *Six Demonstration School Districts* (New York: Praeger, 1968), conclusion.

7. M. Gittell, *Participants and Participation* (New York: Praeger, 1966), pp. 46, 54.

8. For a more detailed discussion of the situation see either Alan Rosenthal, *Pedagogues and Power* (Syracuse: Syracuse University Press, 1969), or C. Myers, *Collective Bargaining for Teachers* (Lexington, Mass.: D.C. Heath, 1972).

9. M. Kirst and F. Wirt, *The Political Web of American Schools* (Boston: Little, Brown, 1972), ch. 4.

10. *Ibid.,* p. 7, reprinted by permission.

11. *Ibid.,* p. 92, reprinted by permission.

12. Rosenthal, *op. cit.*

13. J. Koerner, *Who Controls American Education?* (Boston: Beacon, 1968), ch. 2.

14. *Ibid.,* p. 96.

15. Massachusetts General Laws for 1969.

16. *Ibid.,* ch. 149, section 178G through 178N.

17. Interviews with the superintendents in Melrose and Weston on December 6 and December 9, 1972.

18. Interview with Mr. Ted Phillips, Weston, February 16, 1973.

19. Interviews with the superintendents in Quincy and Wellesley on January 4 and January 2, 1973.

20. Interview with Mr. Paul Kelly, Quincy, January 24, 1973.

21. Interview with Mr. Ted Phillips, *op. cit.*

22. Information from an internal letter from the IPT to the school committee, October 1972.

23. Interview with Mr. Don Mack, President of the MEA, January 10, 1973.

24. Interview with Dr. Goodman, *op. cit.*

25. Interview with Ms. Joan Shaffer, February 27, 1973.

26. Interviews with the four teacher representatives, *op. cit.*

27. *Ibid.*

28. Information from the contract documents for 1972–73.

29. The Weston teacher contract for 1972–73, p. 13.

30. Decision taken at Quincy and minuted for January 10, 1973.

31. Interview with Mr. Francis X. McCauley, Quincy, January 17, 1973.

32. Meetings held on February 8 and February 27, 1973.

33. Interview with Mr. Ted Phillips, *op. cit.*

34. Meetings held in Weston on March 19 and 26, 1973.

35. Interviews with the superintendents, *op. cit.*

36. Interview with Dr. Creedon, *op. cit.*
37. Interview with Dr. Goodman, *op. cit.*
38. Interview with Dr. Creedon, *op. cit.*
39. Interview with Dr. Quin, *op. cit.*
40. M. Kirst and F. Wirt, *op. cit.,* p. 90, reprinted by permission.
41. Interview with Mr. Ed. Barry, Melrose, January 12, 1973.
42. Interview with Dr. Bob Bachelder, Melrose, January 3, 1973.
43. Interviews with Dr. Bob Bachelder, Mr. Bill Phinney, and Dr. Nick Muto, December-January 1973.
44. M. Kirst and F. Wirt, *op. cit.,* p. 90.
45. Interview with Mr. Crowley, *op. cit.*
46. Interview with Mr. Don Mack, *op. cit.*
47. Interview with Ms. Joan Shaffer, *op. cit.*
48. Myers, *op. cit.,* p. 100.
49. M. Kirst and F. Wirt, *op. cit.,* p. 10.
50. Interview with Joan Wexler, February 19, 1973.
51. Alan Rosenthal, *Administrator-Teacher Relationships* In M. Kirst, *op. cit.,* p. 71.
52. *Ibid.,* p. 97.

Chapter Eight

The Effects of Government Machinery

I have discussed interactions between elected representatives, administrators, and the community on the assumption of school district autonomy. Although all four districts have fiscal autonomy, they are not entirely free to choose their own policies. First, they do not operate in a vacuum but rather in the context of municipal government. Secondly, to pursue their policies they require funding because they have no legal powers to raise revenue. They must cooperate with those community representatives elected to provide resources for the supply of government services. The school committees are not without bounds: municipal officials have a formal role in determining educational services.

What is the actual role of the municipal officials? Does it differ according to government machinery? Does one form lead to more citizen influence, whether of representative or lay kind, than another does? To answer these questions, two types of government were chosen—the city and the town. In this chapter I discuss whether the formal machinery had an effect upon citizen participation and sphere of influence. The premise is that it could have an effect at two points, those of process and of outcome. It could also be effective for the whole budget or for just operating or salary issues. There is evidence for the large cities:

> The mayor restricts his area of influence to the overall budget
> ceiling . . . and in some cities to the amount of salary increase for
> the teachers.[1]

MACHINERY FOR MUNICIPAL OFFICIALS

One of the responsibilities of municipal officials is to set the tax rate in order to raise sufficient revenue for all their services. They may, therefore, set budget guidelines or ceilings. They should scrutinize departmental budgets for their possible effects upon the tax rate.[2] Various machinery may be used for review and for ratification.

Official inspections differed between the cities and towns. In the cities the practice was that school committees submit their budgets to the responsible officials—namely, the mayor—prior to a statutory deadline in January of the budget year. The mayor would assess and present the proposals to the officially elected body—city council or board of aldermen—for further examination. Municipal overview would take several weeks, so that budgets would not be finalized until the statutory deadline of April 1st of the budget year. The overview includes a public hearing and an open confirmatory meeting.[3] This process would often necessitate contact between financial body and school committee to clarify the budget total and its implications. But on the whole, the two sets of officials would remain separate, preserving their independence. By custom, the contact would be over the total budget size, rarely over its component parts.

In the towns, the machinery was somewhat different. The tax rate would be set after a vote at the town meeting directed by the town moderator, an elected official. The town meeting is an annual business meeting towards the end of March in which the year's expenditures and policies are decided upon. Recommendations are made by a finance committee appointed for that purpose.

Although the towns' school committees have fiscal autonomy, it is a limited notion. A school committee only has autonomy over its budget if it is submitted to the town meeting before the statutory date. If the estimates of expenditure need to be revised from those voted on at the town meeting, the school committee has to request an appropriation, which requires a vote at a special town meeting. The two school committees observed do not usually exert their powers of fiscal autonomy. They cooperate with the team of financial officials to reach a consensus on the appropriate budget figure. Indeed, a subcommittee of the officials has been created in each of the towns studied with the specific function of inspecting the education budget; this is a manifestation of cooperative behavior.[4] In fact, the school budget in Weston is two-thirds the total town budget; in Wellesley education constitutes over half.[5]

MUNICIPAL INTERACTION AND DELIBERATION

There was an overt relationship between the municipal officials and the school committee in Quincy. The mayor sits as chairman of the school committee, and therefore attends all the budget sessions, including negotiations. There was more than close collaboration because the mayor was involved as a member in the decision-making process. He did not issue early guidelines. To provide information to the city councillors the mayor also set up a budget review committee and employed a budget manager.[6] As a result of this independent review, the mayor tried to change several of the superintendent's proposals during deliberations on the operating budget.[7] His first objective was to cut out certain items, especially plant renovations and operation. However, he did not succeed in persuading the committee; the superintendent's proposals were, in the main, accepted. His second objective was to reduce the burden on the tax rate caused by the 18-month budget. He therefore tried to change the purchasing pattern of the school department and, to this end, called in the purchasing manager to a committee meeting.[8] He succeeded in convincing it, and eventually the professional educators, of the efficiency of his proposals. He pointed out that it would not "hurt" the school system. A sum of less than 1 percent was eventually removed from the budget estimate as a result of the mayor's proposals. The mayor employed a very explicit and clear strategy. He did not want to interfere with the educational process. He was concerned with the costs of the school system and its consequent business practices. He therefore avoided looking into the operation of the instructional programs, commenting, "I leave the academic end to the professional educators. My biggest job is fiscal responsibility."[9]

Apart from the mayor, the financial officials in Quincy did not get involved in the process of deliberation or negotiations. However, several committee members emphatically pointed out that the city council was invited to attend budget meetings since they were all open to the public.[10] There were no other formal channels available for communication. The city council wanted the school committee to attend its annual budget review and public hearing. The members refused since the school committee had open meetings and its own public hearing. They made the excuse that they wanted to preserve committee autonomy. Above all, the committee had invited the city council to its meetings, and the council had chosen not to respond. The budgetary process, in fact, was not exactly one of collaboration between the municipal officials and the school committee. The incursions upon the superintendent's work were restricted to technical or administrative matters and did not relate to the instructional programs. The sphere of influence of the mayor and his officials was clearly bounded: it did extend over all financial issues. The council had to appropriate a special amount for salary contracts in 1972. The 1973-4 contracts also were not settled by the statutory deadline.

In Melrose the whole budgetary process was conducted without the involvement of any municipal officials. The mayor was not entitled to a seat on the school committee.[11] He did not set guidelines until budget deliberations began, and then he did not attend any meetings, nor did the board of aldermen have any formal contact with the school committee. The mayor, however, was kept informed of the committee proposals through personal contact.[12] The only participation observed was that of the municipal officials at the public hearing because the committee had ignored the guidelines.[13] Several aldermen and the mayor attended and posed questions with budgetary implications: the long-term issue of school population size and its relation to school policies such as plant needs and the pupil-teacher ratio. At the public hearing certain points such as these were made:

> We have already dropped 700 pupils in 7 years. The numbers going to the parochial schools are less than before but insignificant. We therefore hit zero population growth a month ago. . . . I suggest that the staffing be fewer than last year . . . so I hope it will come up in the Aldermen's review. There are already empty rooms in the elementary schools . . . . you should not drift into decreasing class size without planning. . . .[14]

However, the committee did not then address these questions and change the budget estimates. During their evaluation of the budgets, the aldermen continued to comment publicly about the declining school population and the need to economize on professional personnel. This was after the school committee had endorsed its budget. At the same time the school committee, on receipt of an administrative reorganization proposal from the superintendent, decided to review its total staffing complement.[15] It found that it could indeed make certain savings by eliminating some administrative positions and five teaching posts.

Therefore, the aldermen did have an indirect effect upon the budget total. They also talked publicly about negotiations in an attempt to affect salary increases. They also tried to have a direct effect by proposing a meeting with the school committee to discuss the operating budget. The committee was loathe to accept, but finally did so because it regarded the step as a necessary exercise in public relations.[16] At that meeting the aldermen went through some of the budget details such as staffing, pupil-teacher ratio, administration, and the overall figure due to declining enrollments. After conflict among themselves, they asked for a further cut of 2 percent in the school budget. The school committee was very defensive and talked about the technical complications of so doing and their educational philosophy. The committee did agree to inspect the budget again but would offer no promises of such a cut. In fact, they were able to make changes in staffing but not in the same proportion as the aldermen had proposed.[17] They agreed to collaborate with the aldermen in order to preserve for the public at least a semblance of being "fiscally responsible." They did achieve some reductions. Again, the sphere of influence of the municipal officials was clear. It was in general, rather than specifically, educational areas and was basically related to the total budget figure and not its components. Parts of the budget that were discussed concerned types of resources, such as personnel, and not actual appropriations. The questions were not directed at the actual educational programs. Moreover, the officials were involved in ratifying the salary increases and appropriating an extra amount for the 1972–3 contract as a result of prolonged negotiations. They did not veto the increase.

In summary, the two cities were not dissimilar over school committee and municipal official relations. Both committees tried to retain their separate spheres of influence but acknowledged the need for collaboration to reach a publicly acceptable agreement on budget size. The discussions covered politically sensitive but not specific educational topics. Their similar areas of intervention were implicitly acknowledged; the actual procedures differed.

The two towns also had some agreement, over procedure rather than content. Wellesley's substantive behavior was a contrast not only with Weston but also the two cities. Both town school committees did hold several meetings with the financial advisors. The financial subcommittee also attended all the open school meetings. There was complete official collaboration throughout. In Wellesley, this was because of strong differences of opinion between the two committees over the proposed budget total. The school committee felt bound to respond to the advisors. In Weston, collaboration was customary and this year was mere ritual.

Wellesley's committee met twice with the advisory committee, at the beginning and the end of the operating budget process.[18] Its subcommittee attended all open and closed school committee meetings. The first meeting with the advisory committee was for the school committee to announce its intentions. A similar process occurred usually for salary negotiations. It had happened the previous spring before the two-year contract was settled. But the actual discussion here was not purely financial; members of the advisory committee volunteered suggestions about school policies. The school committee met with the subcommittee to discuss the superintendent's proposals in private sessions. The Wellesley chairman claimed:

> I try to be sympathetic to those with no kids in school. The school committee are supposed to reflect what the town wants to the superintendent and yet half the people in town have no kids in school . . . . There used to be a hostile atmosphere here . . . . I've tried to change that by working with the advisory committee . . . even the *Townsman* [the local paper] praised us for keeping the budget down . . . .[19]

The purpose was to argue over cutting down the size of the budget.[20] The outcome was that a committee member raised the elementary schools' problem as a way of altering the budget increase. This choice was a result not only of the advisory committee but also the influence of a selectman.[21] After three open committee meetings, the reduction of the budget increase still had not been resolved to the satisfaction of the advisory committee. Alternate means had to be sought. More pressure was exerted, and three more school and advisory committee work sessions held. A consensus was hard to obtain because the members had different motives for being officials. First, the subcommittee suggested changes in business practice and plant operation. As a result, the committee agreed not to renovate certain buildings. This still did not reduce the budget total sufficiently. Therefore, two school members pressed for numerical detail on personnel and equipment from the superintendent in order to check on their adequacy.[22] The superintendent was loathe to provide it, and the committee concurred with his definition of their responsibilities. It therefore asked him to cut down on equipment. Again, the subcommittee was not satisfied, and wanted particular cuts to educational frills. After a long and heated debate lasting over several weeks, the committee agreed with the advisors to dispense with the frills. Because of a related school problem, it took the superintendent's recommendation, reached only with difficulty.

> I do mind the cuts but politically the most important thrust is the advisory committee support. In fact we made a tactical error in the definition of the summer workshops. If we hadn't we would not have had the argument.[23]

The school committee wanted a high school addition and needed support in the town meeting to get it. Advisory committee recommendations to the town meeting were therefore crucial. The addition was given higher priority than the educational frills. The school committee therefore acceded to the subcommittee's demands, but not without some regret. The superintendent added this comment:

> The Advisory Committee should say whether the dollars are too much—they should not look at programs. The most distressing part of the process this year is the cuts they propose.[24]

When the committee presented its budget to the advisory committee for final endorsement, it knew that this budget would have an easy passage. The meeting indeed was amazingly short, lasting little over an hour. As a result, the advisory committee gave full support to the budget at the public hearing and the town meeting.

Wellesley's interactions demonstrate a different aspect of municipal involvement from that in Quincy and Melrose. The finance committee was certainly involved in substantive decisions on the operating budget. It did not restrict itself to costs alone but discussed the merits of educational policies. This did not happen in the two cities. Furthermore, the subcommittee behaved like an extension of the school committee, attending all meetings. It was only at the public meetings that it did not appear to be a partner of equal standing. From the substance of the debate it appears that it was.

A number of explanations could be advanced to account for the difference between Wellesley and the two cities. It may be explained in terms of government machinery. The town form allowed for more communication and therefore actual interaction. Or political culture, the relations between various community groups, may be apposite. The latter seems most appropriate, for the town's municipal activities were not as rigidly separate as those of the cities, given the representation of citizens. To get a clearer sense of the more convincing explanation, let us turn to Weston, the other town.

Weston's school committee also met frequently with its finance committee and its subcommittee for education. Several work sessions were held, and the subcommittee attended all the open budget sessions. None of the sessions was characterized by conflict as in Wellesley. The subcommittee was given an explanation of the operating budget, page by page, and salary negotiations. Its main concern was with the proportion to be allocated to the teachers' salary increase. The expense budget was summarily dismissed. The school committee met with the full advisory committee twice. Each became a dialogue between the two chairmen on strategies of collective bargaining.[25] The committees did agree to fix on an estimate of the increase, which would be written into the proposed budget in such a way that the teachers would be unable to discern it. The school chairman was eventually convinced that this would not harm his negotiations with the teachers and that it was in the public interest. Thus the committee agreed, on the resolution of the high school program changes, to support the school budget at the public hearing and the town meeting.

APPROACHES TO FINANCIAL INVOLVEMENT

In all four communities there were different procedures and interventions. Government form is not adequate since the towns differed over content and cities over procedure. There is a definite patterning. Three were similar in type of intervention, if not procedure. They all wished to maintain publicly the status quo in municipal relations. The operations were not very significant. The financial officials did not have a tremendous impact upon the actual decisions. In Quincy, for example, less than 1 percent of the operating budget was altered. In Melrose the proportion was approximately the same, achieved more surreptitiously through indirect influence. In Weston, less of the budget was affected because the officials' influence was informal and in the preparatory stages. The deliberations, although lengthy, constituted rhetoric. They were keyed to a particular issue—the budget increase. In this, the school committee also accepted advice for negotiations.

In Wellesley the deliberations were more significant and direct. The finance committee succeeded in removing a specific item—equipment— which was almost 2 percent of the budget proposal. It pointed to specifics rather than totals. Other items removed were not peripheral to the educational

program: they were dubbed as educational frills. Nevertheless, the advisory
committee involved itself in determining the content of the school budget. The
chairman of the advisory subcommittee admitted:

> It is a little bit against the rules, so to speak. There was a lot of
> wrangling . . . . the school committee took no position at first . . .
> and they felt it perfectly in order for us to do so . . . . The advisory
> committee look from outside is very practical . . . . The school
> committee have not enforced fiscal autonomy . . . . They have
> respected our criticism . . . .[26]

The chairman of the school committee had a different opinion:

> We have excellent school-advisory committee relations. I don't
> want fiscal autonomy. Only one thing bothered me. In the final
> analysis the advisory committee pointed to specific items that they
> wanted out. It is against my philosophy . . . . we should choose.
> They have no way of knowing the relative importance of the items.
> I finally agreed for the sake of harmony. If they did it again I'd
> reverse my opinion of fiscal autonomy.[27]

The reason for the differences in the involvement of municipal
officials cannot be explained in terms of machinery. The two towns behaved
very distinctively. Nor is size an adequate explanation since the smaller town
was more similar to the cities. What is a more plausible explanation is community
political and social characteristics. The Wellesley community is much less
politically homogeneous than either Melrose or Weston. It is probably rather
more homogeneous than Quincy in terms of socioeconomic variables, but its
range of political interests is more varied. Added to this, the demographic
distribution of the Wellesley population, like that in Quincy, is more spread
out than in Weston, both having a high proportion of older citizens. (This was
shown in Table 3-5.) More importantly, this distribution is reflected in the
political representation of the Wellesley community. This was not the case in
Quincy in 1972-3. The selectmen, advisory committee, and town meeting
members in Wellesley were descriptively, if not formally, representative of the
older and wealthier citizens whose children had already graduated from the
schools. (Descriptive representation refers to the similarity of social and demographic characteristics of the representatives and the community, rather than
the more usual notion of similarity in terms of political attitudes. It refers more
to attributes.[28]) The personal and political concerns of these citizens extended
beyond the quality of the local school system. The school committee represented those with interests in the schools. Their personal interests were obviously
different from the other representatives who were concerned with community
amenities and, more crucially, with the town's level of spending. Conflicts

arose between these sets of interests. These conflicts had been characteristic of Wellesley's educational and political process for many years. The task of formulating an acceptable budget for the entire community was very difficult for the superintendent. The committees tended to display an adversary style of behavior. The superintendent chose not to be directive of the school committee, but presented a budget for them specifically. This was not agreeable to the advisory committee, and conflict inevitably arose. If the superintendent had been more frugal, cautious, and wary of the advisory committee, he might have avoided the committees' confrontation. But the task was supremely difficult.

The three other superintendents had less difficult assignments. In Melrose there was only a mild tradition of conflict between the aldermen and the school committee. The latter had usually held the superior position because of the legal consequences attaching to threats to fiscal autonomy that the aldermen might make. Even though the school committees were becoming more cautious because of the changing climate of opinion regarding fiscal autonomy, their caution affected the situation only marginally. In Weston there was no tradition of conflict, but one of implicit faith in the school committee to adopt a budget oriented to a "lighthouse" educational system. The finance committee, also representing citizens with children in the public schools, wanted, in common with the school committee, a quality education system. They therefore only haggled about absolute costs. In Quincy there had not been a real conflict between the city council and the school committee, although the two committees did not usually represent the same interests. In 1972–3, however, the school committee was more descriptively representative of the same interests as the city council. For instance, only one member of the committee had children in the public schools. The two committees essentially had the same outlook toward fiscal responsibility and used an adversary mode of behavior. The superintendent's tasks were less difficult than those of Wellesley's superintendent. (However, the tasks were perhaps less enviable in professional terms. The Quincy superintendent was allowed less flexibility in spending and a much smaller per pupil expenditure. In 1971 the Quincy per pupil cost was $919 and Wellesley $1,254, which is 36 percent more.)

Rather than size, the differences in the decision-making process over salary and operating budget may be accounted for by a combination of the community's political characteristics and superintendent strategies. Wellesley's superintendent precipitated conflict; it was not inevitable that he would do it, but it was more difficult to avoid than in the other communities. Government machinery does not necessarily affect participation although it may, depending upon the community's representatives. Even so, the municipal officials limit their influence to that of finance and total costs. In Quincy and Melrose the committees tried to contain the actual demands for ceilings on negotiations. In Weston and Wellesley, usually the committees were more willing to act within the guidelines. The part played by the professional educators is crucial to this. It is vital how the formal mechanisms are manipulated. This manipulation is even more pertinent to the budget outcomes.

CITY FORM VERSUS TOWN MEETING

The implications of government machinery extend over process and outcome. It is yet possible that the machinery could affect public participation over final decisions. Indeed, government form is critical here, for the major differences are in forms of representative democracy. The town meeting is based on the concept of direct democracy: citizens are invited to attend and are provided with information for decisions. Town citizens, at least, have a lot of knowledge about the decisions that are being taken. They are automatically given a wealth of literature. Citizens may actually participate in the final stages of decision. In the cities, citizens are not given special opportunities to examine the final budget carefully. They may attend the budget reviews as audience, but their representatives make the decisions.

In Wellesley there are 240 town meeting members. In March of 1973, most of them were present for the discussion of the educational budget. There were about that many citizens present who were observing. In Weston almost 500 citizens—5 percent of the town—attended the town meeting at which the school budget was presented. Attendance at meetings is a very limited indicator of influence, if not participation. As regards influence, the school budgets were not important in the town meeting debates. In Weston the budget was briefly presented by the committee chairman. It was instantly voted on, with no questions raised, and passed unanimously, before a half hour of the meeting had transpired. This could indicate public apathy or lack of ability to have an impact upon the budget and its administration. This meeting may not be the relevant forum to change budget decisions, but is more likely to indicate satisfaction with the school system in this case, given prior evidence of the limited kinds of pressures exerted.

In Wellesley the school budget was also presented at the first session of the town meeting, with virtually all 240 members present. About six questions were raised, all pertaining to the 18-month factor and the payment of teachers' salaries. Explanations were provided that did not entirely satisfy all the town meeting members. But the budget was voted on and passed in that very evening. No other questions were even raised. The town meeting did not make for public influence over the decisions taken. The public, presumably, had their interests cared for by the school committee or the municipal officials prior to these meetings.

The citizens could not, obviously, be influential. The meetings were, however, important in that they indicated some level of public interest in the political if not the educational process. To that extent, there was evidence of more public participation in educational decision-making than in the cities. But participants' influence in the actual town meeting was more an illusion than a reality. Budgets, formulated by the professional educators, are customarily accepted. This was the case in Weston. It was in Wellesley that the budget created a stir. The reason was plain: the superintendent had miscalculated the locus of community consensus on an acceptable tax rate increase. He had though predicted that the advisory committee would not automatically accept his budget proposals.

SUMMARY

There is little difference in the effect that government machinery has on the actual decisions. Three of the four committees were similar. The decisions are formulated by the superintendent and ratified summarily. The differences between the communities occur if the superintendent is in a factional community and one that is not adequately represented over a range of opinions.[29] The onus is on the superintendent to prepare for the community. If he calculates correctly, he gets little flack. Given the formal machinery, there is always the potential for lay citizen participation and intervention by municipal representatives. It is not manifest unless interests are ill catered for. In the case of Wellesley they were. The attitudes in all the communities are the same toward the social division of labor. The roles of professional educator and public officials are accepted; they run the systems. The differences in citizen behavior occur only when there are violations through incompetence or misunderstanding. As Banfield states, "Civil servants may have much influence but may be checked by elected officials whose cooperation is essential."[30]

Citizen involvement may be manifest in various settings. It is likely to be related to the attitudes that committee members have toward public office. Involvement probably happened in Wellesley precisely because of the committee's adversary mode of behavior, a consequence of fiscal concern. It was also the mode of the advisory. Quincy's committee could also have sparked off community conflicts since such are reputed to have occurred in the recent past.

Why, then, does government machinery, especially the town form, have only a small effect upon process or outcomes and in limited areas? The most plausible explanation is that acceptance of the social division of labor is pervasive. It means acceptance of individual responsibility for a social task, whether or not it requires a complex skill. The nature of citizen assembly is not clearly understood. A citizen assembly, to make community decisions, violates these general standards of demarcated responsibilities.[31] Citizens, not imbued with an understanding of political involvement cannot use the machinery. Those school and town meeting representatives who take part have a high sense of personal self-efficacy and have learned, probably through work experience, that they are able to play an effective part in such decisions. However, few citizens are socialized into this form of behavior. Therefore, the town meeting was more a caricature of the annual general meeting of a business corporation than an example of overt citizen involvement in the management of community affairs. It is such an anachronism in the now conventional governmental process that it is not used by the majority of citizens. The apathy that appears to be characteristic of other levels of public participation prevails. In fact, apathy may be a function of socialization rather than indifference or lack of interest. Indeed, the principle of representation may have been effective to the extent that citizen views are taken care of in the earlier stages of budgeting so that there is no need for any involvement over final decisions. The town meetings, which did not differ essentially in the two towns, may have a symbolic importance. The community is aware of the machinery available for citizen influence. It has no real value in that it cannot be used adequately.

Municipal officials do have some formal opportunities to affect process and outcome by making statements throughout the budget deliberation. Government form has little effect. The differences observed related to the effectiveness with which the superintendents operate and to committee evaluations of their competence. Although there is some citizen input into the process through the municipal officials as representatives, it is not very great. On the whole, the officials' sphere of influence relates to the total budget or to its proportionate change rather than to substance or component parts. The superintendent and the school committee are left relatively free to determine educational content. The mystique of educational professionalism holds sway. But with regard to technical problems and managerialism, the local government officials are not slow to interfere. The domains of the public officials are clearly delineated; and both sets of officials know well the areas of work in which they may legitimately intervene. The community also accepts these definitions.

NOTES TO CHAPTER EIGHT

1. M. Kirst, *The Politics of Education at the Local, State and Federal Levels* (Berkeley: McCutchan, 1970), p. 7.
2. In fact, all municipalities elect or appoint a special committee for the purpose of this scrutiny, according to their own statutes.
3. See, for example, Melrose, Revised Ordinances 1956; or the City Charter of Quincy for the rules of this procedure.
4. By 1972, the Wellesley subcommittee had been in existence for six years; in Weston, over three years.
5. See Table 2–2.
6. Interview with Mr. Walter Hannon, Quincy's mayor, January 18, 1973.
7. He proposed several changes to the budget at the meetings in Quincy on January 4, 10, and 25, 1973.

8. Quincy committee meeting on January 10, 1973.
9. Interview with Mr. Walter Hannon, *op. cit.*
10. Interview with Mr. Daniel Raymondi and Mr. Harold Davis on January 18, 1973. The sentiment was also expressed at several school committee meetings in Quincy.
11. Revised City Ordinances of Melrose, 1956.
12. Interview with the Melrose superintendent, January 3, 1973.
13. The public hearing was held at the Beebe Elementary School auditorium, Melrose, on January 3, 1973.
14. Alderman Alley, *ibid.*
15. The Melrose school committee received the revised reorganization proposal at their meeting on February 26, 1973.
16. The meeting was held on a Saturday, March 10, 1973.
17. Details sent from the chairman of the school committee, Mr. Paul Butler and the superintendent to the Aldermen on March 20, 1973.
18. The Wellesley meetings were held on December 4, 1972, and February 8, 1973.
19. Interview with Mr. David McNeish of Wellesley, in Boston, on February 13, 1973.
20. Interview with the Wellesley superintendent, January 2, 1973.
21. Report of David Sargent's speech in the *Townsman,* Wellesley's local newspaper, December 29, 1972.
22. Reported in interviews with Ms. Jean Kelly in Wellesley, February 16, 1973, and Mr. Bob Hoffman, chairman of the Advisory subcommittee, on February 14, 1973.
23. Interview with Dr. Goodman, February 8, 1973.
24. *Ibid.*
25. The meetings in Weston were held on February 8, 1973, and February 27, 1973.
26. Interview with Mr. Bob Hoffman, *op. cit.*
27. Interview with Mr. David McNeish, *op. cit.*
28. See Hannah Pitkin, *The Concept of Representation.* (Berkeley: California University Press, 1967), pp. 60–91.
29. The term "factional" was used by D. McCarty and J.E. Ramsey to classify communities that were not pluralistic but contained several competing and active interest groups. See D. McCarty and J.E. Ramsey, *The School Managers* (Newport, Ct.: Greenwood, 1971), part 3.
30. E. Banfield, *Political Influence* (New York: The Free Press, 1961), p. 7.
31. For a fuller discussion see Jane J. Mansbridge, *Town Meeting Democracy.* In *Working Papers for a New Society,* Vols. 1, No. 2, pp. 5–13., summer 1973.

Chapter Nine

Conclusions

In the foregoing chapters I have explored the spheres of influence that various participants have in budgeting in local school districts. The main questions addressed were whether there was more citizen participation and influence in small school districts than in the larger ones, and more evidence of citizen participation in the towns than in the cities where the formal opportunities for participation if not influence are greater; and as a consequence, what the components of educational professionalism were. Although this study looked only at the evidence from four school districts and one year of the budgetary process, the data are such that the conclusions are clear. I have found little evidence of continuous lay citizen participation and influence in any of the school districts. What occurs is sporadic reactions to changes in the status quo. Nor is there much evidence of actual influence by representatives, whether school or municipal, on the budgetary process. Here the influences exerted related to the size of budget increase, either for operations or salary, and not the component parts.

The main source of influence on the decisions taken on the budget in that one year is the school superintendent, a professional educator. However, his influence is not unbounded. It draws strength from its roots in the character of the local community. I did not, therefore, find a uniform approach to educational decision-making, although the chief characteristic is its tendency towards professional rather than citizen control. What emerges from the study is that professionalism has a strong impact in all the four school districts. The interpretation of professionalism varies from district to district. The variations in mode of behavior cannot be explained by size or government machinery but are more easily interpreted as manifestations of the organizational or stylistic idiosyncracies of each community's political culture. This conclusion supports the evidence from other studies about educational decision-making, even though it is in the area of financial decisions and the presumption was that they would be of a different ilk from purely educational decisions.[1]

Substantial control of the budgetary process lies with the professional educators. This does not mean a wide group of individuals. The school superintendent and his immediate colleagues are the ones with whom the main initiatives for the decisions lie. The occupations within education do not make up a homogeneous profession. Other interest groups who may also be termed professional educators, such as teachers and administrators, do not have the prerogative to influence the whole process, although they may influence that part which relates to their self-interests. The superintendent does not define them as having the same community of interest as himself. As a corollary, they do not see themselves with the same set of interests as the superintendent. There is no inclusive or comprehensive concept of the profession of educators. Splits occur according to the client systems which the component occupational groups serve.

The school superintendent, although able to define his professional interests in the budget, is constrained in his choices of specific changes by the social and political context in which he operates. He is primarily accountable to the school committee, and if he does not define his own interests in terms that are compatible with the committee, his influence will immediately erode. He may indeed be fired. With regard to financial decisions, the school representatives whom the superintendent serves are not solely responsible. The community also elects representatives whose chief task is the level of public expenditure and the allocation of financial resources for all municipal services. The superintendent has also to be mindful of community wishes on topics other than education as expressed by the municipal officials. It seemed intuitively obvious that in this context the superintendent would have very little freedom to control the situation and would rely on the directives of the community. However, most financial decisions are fixed from year to year, and much of the expenditure of the community is on recurrent items such as instructional programs or buildings. Changes are at the margins, innovations or deletions, to contain any budget increase which would increase the tax rate. In this area it is indeed the superintendent who initiates the changes. He does so on the basis of his personal judgment of the community and its requirements. He cannot be termed an "unmoved mover"; the notion of a non-decision process also seems apposite.[2]

The basic approach of the school committee may be summarized as "The superintendent recommends; the school committee votes."[3] The school committees do not see it as proper that they take the initiatives. Size of community does not affect the attitudes or behavior of committee members in this context. In the smaller school districts the members do not take any more actions to determine the budget than they do in the larger school districts; they do not solicit opinions from the community more frequently than is the case in

the larger. Nor does small size mean that the committee provides more opportunities for citizen participation. Indeed, the attitudes of the committee members towards their role as public officials and towards the inclusion of the
citizens in the budgetary process do not differ between the large and small
communities. It is that as representatives they should act as trustees of the
school system, preventing the superintendent from acting when they see his
actions as inappropriate. They expect similar behavior from lay citizens and
therefore do not provide extensive opportunities for lay citizen involvement.
Indeed, lay citizens do not make many contributions, and there is no difference
in input on the basis of community size. The inputs were over changes in the
status quo, and they were responded to. The committees are not oblivious to
pressure from the citizens. For example, even in a year of financial stringency,
both Quincy and Wellesley agreed against the superintendents' initial advice
to implement the state-mandated lunch program. Admittedly, by a curious
coincidence they were the last two school districts in the state to agree to the
program.

       There are two caveats to this general statement about the behavior
of the school committee. The first is that in regard to salary negotiations, size
does seem of marginal importance to patterns of behavior in process, if not in
outcome. However, in this area, the definition of professional educator is rather
different from that of the operating budget. In this case, the control of the system is in an uneasy tension between administrators and teachers. There is a
different emphasis in school committee interactions with the professional
educators. Negotiations take place between the committee and teachers.

       Given that point, in the two smaller communities, the committees
behaved slightly differently from the larger. Wellesley and Weston's professional
employees had not yet developed a large-scale organization. Professional control therefore implied control by both the teachers and some administrators
together, rather than merely the teachers, as was the case in Quincy and Melrose.
It still did not include the superintendent and his immediate staff. Size may
not be the essence. There may be another explanation, which can only be offered
tentatively, which is that the differences of interest of the occupational ranks
in the educational profession do not appear to be so great in Wellesley and
Weston because they are wealthier communities. The issue with which they are
concerned is salary. All the educators are paid better in these two communities
then they are in Quincy and Melrose, and there is therefore less reason to be
engaged in disputes with the school committee or between ranks in the profession. Wealth of the community rather than size is therefore probably more
important. In any event, in all four districts there were serious differences of
interest generally between the superintendent and the ranks of administrator
and teacher. It was the line of demarcation within the local ranks of the educational profession that differed among the four communities.

       Second, Wellesley's behavior differed from that of the other districts.

Although Wellesley's committee members all held attitudes similar to those of the other committee members, they did not actually behave in like manner. They did initiate some activity that the superintendent had not suggested as part of the budget review. They did solicit opinions from the community on certain issues that pertained to the budget. But they did not do so systematically; rather, they selected out some critical problems. The explanation for this behavior cannot be the relative size of the district. Weston and Melrose did not behave in like manner although they, too, did instigate some citizen participation. Their initiatives were not of the same magnitude as that in Wellesley.

Size does not have an impact upon the extent of citizen influence. It does not explain the observed variation between the four school districts, most of which is attributable to Wellesley. The second question was that form of government machinery would discriminate over citizen participation and influence. There is indeed a difference in participation between the four school districts, particularly as manifest by the financial officials. Since Weston's machinery was the same as Wellesley's, the relationship between participation and government form could only hold true if the two towns exhibited the same type of behavior. They did not. In Weston the machinery was used only in ritualistic fashion by the school committee and not in a way that allowed the finance committee strong influence. In Wellesley the school committee allowed the advisory committee to participate and actually influence the budget outcomes. There was considerably more participation by the municipal officials in Wellesley than in Weston. It was greater than in the two cities, Quincy and Melrose. The three latter, in fact, exhibited similar behavior. Moreover, the committee members in these three communities also expressed similar attitudes towards their relationship with other municipal officials. They regarded fiscal autonomy as a reality; and to that extent, it was. In fact, for all four school committees it may not have been: the three committees may have learned to use a working relationship that avoided conflicts and confrontations about the proper financial relationships between the two bodies of community representatives. The study addressed the question of how the budget was decided in practice. The evidence points to the fact that there was little influence, if not participation, from the financial officials. But the potentiality of their influence did exist. It was realized in practice for the 1973-4 budget, only with regard to a budget ceiling, and already tacitly agreed upon in the three communities. So changes in budget proposals were small.

Moreover, the various governmental mechanisms such as the town meetings did not particularly affect budget decisions overtly. Although the citizens present, and there were a great many, did not affect the decisions taken, they could have done so if they had chosen to. The government machinery provided formal opportunities since it was based on the principle of direct rather than representative democracy. It therefore provided the means, at least for the community's representatives and superintendent, to assess the general mood toward spending. It also provided a safety valve for citizens if they were discontented, and as such, did have symbolic significance. What seems clear is that forms of government machinery within one type of society, covering both financial and general political arrangements, do not affect the extent of actual citizen participation.

There is an exception to this general conclusion. In the area of collective bargaining, there was a small difference in influence based on form of government. In the towns the financial officials did give definitive advice on salary increases, which was accepted by the school committees. In the cities the advice was proferred and only grudgingly regarded. The influence, however, did not amount to overall control of the process of negotiations and was in the narrow area of finance. It had nothing to do with educational priorities. The advice was readily accepted in Wellesley and Weston because the finance committees were making a stand on the equity between certain classes of occupation. The position they were taking did not clash with the attitude of the school committees toward the teachers. The stand was also related to the general problem of the appropriate budget increase that the school committee would be allowed as compared with the other departments of the local government. The area of influence of the municipal bodies was clearly financial and not educational.

Differences in behavior have been noted between the four school committees at two levels: first, that of eliciting lay citizen participation and contributions and, second, actual school committee behavior and interaction with the superintendent over the deliberations and budget outcomes. The attitudes of both the school administrators and the committee members tend to be in the same direction—acceptance of a notion of professionalism. The two variables presumed to affect this—size and governmental style—do not explain the differences in behavior. What, then, does? With regard to lay citizen participation, Wellesley did not behave like the other three districts because of its actual political representatives and their relations. Its municipal officials, de facto, represent different facets of the community.[4] The officials who are generally influential in the community and regarded as prestigious are the advisory committee and selectmen. There is a constant conflict between these official bodies who are responsible for the town's general conduct and the school committee on appropriate levels of spending. The conflict could be contained in any year if the school committee sought a compromise with the other officials and was willing to forego its autonomy. But it did not compromise this year; and yet it did not cling to its fiscal autonomy. It followed the general strategy laid out by the superintendent. The result: conflict broke out.

In other districts the differences are less stark between the actual representatives and the constituencies they serve on the various municipal bodies. The greatest potential for similar conflict is in Quincy. In past years, conflicts between the city council and school committee have occurred because the latter did actually represent chiefly school interests. But in the year 1972–3, as a result of the change in elected representatives, the school committee no longer solely represented school interests but was characteristic of the more exclusively "financially responsible" interests in the city. These views were similar to those held by the city councillors. The two bodies were able to act in a sort of harmony, and both clearly acknowledged the superintendent's part in educational matters, a result of his positive strategy.

In Melrose and Weston, fairly homogeneous communities, the municipal and school officials have not come into conflict about the purposes of their actions. The national trends toward fiscal concern had not been fully reflected in the actual elected representatives in these two communities.[5]

The tactics adopted by the superintendents over budget proposals vary depending upon their perception of the local community. The usual behavior and values of the community and its representatives are the foundation on which the superintendent builds. In Wellesley the superintendent, having been appointed to serve the school committee, mistook the significance of the value conflicts between the various officials or at least attempted to ignore it. But he did not succeed. In Quincy the superintendent successfully managed to present a budget that did not open up conflicts between officials. In any case, he had to adopt different tactics for the school committee itself since it had four new members. Because of their political views, the old methods to which this superintendent adhered were no longer sufficient.* He had to find clear justifications for his professional interest in avoiding instructional matters.

The superintendents' strategies are based on their views of their own role as professional educator or administrator. The two superintendents in Quincy and Wellesley emphasized different aspects of their professional roles. The Quincy superintendent was most avowedly an educator and constantly told his committee of his main responsibility which was the instructional programs. The Melrose superintendent was similar. This meant that these two committees—Quincy and Melrose—had areas of the budget in which they could legitimately and easily intervene. The Wellesley superintendent was more interested in management generally than in education matters specifically. He wanted to improve upon the organization of the system but did not take a directive course of action. He left more room for school committee maneuvering and possible influence over budget changes. As a consequence, he opened up the potential internal committee conflict and also conflict with the municipal

---

*Indeed, the superintendent had become very defensive about his tactics. In a letter dated July 6, 1973, commenting on a shorter draft of this study, he claimed that education had to be run by professionals: this was self-evident. He then went on to provide a 50-page critique of my study in which he accused me of a biased position against professionalism. He then stated that he did provide opportunities for citizen participation and that he did not direct the committee members, although education should be run by professionals.

officials. The superintendent in Quincy was able to contain this by his clear strategy.

McCarty and Ramsey attempted a classification of superintendent behavior on the basis of community characteristics.[6] This analysis does not adequately relate to the situations in Quincy and Wellesley. It would seem that these two communities are what they would term "factional" and that the consequent behavior of the superintendent should be that of a political strategist. Indeed, it is true that the two superintendents in some respects were strategists. But the strategies did not preclude superintendent behavior also being that of professional advisor, decision-maker, or functionary. In fact, from this study it appears that the three categories—functionary, advisor, and strategist—are subsets of the general one of decision-maker. This form of super-intendent behavior is the one that emerges with various manifestations in this study where the community characteristics vary. Melrose's superintendent, serving what could be categorized as an "inert" community, behaved more like the superintendent in Quincy than did Wellesley's. The conclusion here is that the superintendent's strategies develop from the organizational situation in which they find themselves rather than from the community's political and socioeconomic characteristics alone. They are not necessarily functionally equivalent to these characteristics. The choices derive from an existential dilemma about the complexity of constraints such as relations between the school com-mittee and municipal officials or the lay citizens. The superintendents have some freedom of choice. The organizational context not only constrains them, but is also determined in part by them.

The variations in superintendent behavior also do not just relate to committee attitudes. The relations between school committees and their superintendents are not functionally equivalent. The actual superintendent strategies did not result in, or totally result from, committee attitudes to their own behavior. The school committee reactions over budget review are to the superintendent's general professional role and not its stylistic manifestations. The reactions are grounded in the motives that the elected members have for serving as public officials. The outcome of the budget process may be summarized by the dynamic interactions between the superintendent and his committee. The actual committee mode of behavior itself may vary, depending upon the attitudes of the elected members to being public officials, accentuated by the chairman's particular role.

The attitudes taken by the members towards being officials help to explain the mode of decision-making within the school committee. In the two districts where concern with fiscal responsibility was paramount—Quincy and Wellesley—a particular stance was taken with regard to the superintendent. Although the members still only reviewed the work of the superintendent, they did so in the critical fashion. They quizzed and probed. They used an *adversary* model, that of the American judicial system. Their acceptance of the superintendent's recommendations was tentative and dependent upon the constant reaffirmation of the competence of the superintendent. The way in which the decisions are taken by the school committee may be termed "neutral" legitimation to denote the caution with which these committee members proceed.[7]

The prevailing mode of behavior in the other two committees—Melrose and Weston—was predicated on a different set of values and therefore resulted in a different set of practices. The members of these committees were not as concerned with costs as they were with education per se. They were interested in running the school system. The way they chose to supervise the superintendent was to respect his wishes and give him firm support. They based their practices on a "business management" model and were *collegial.* They treated the superintendent as their chief executive and therefore the managing director of the system. They endorsed his recommendations and gave him "positive" legitimation.

The attitudes, however different, do not lead to more or less influence. They are all held to acceptance of the notion of professional expertise. None of the committee members wants to take the initiatives in decision-making. They accept the superintendent's definition of their responsibilities: that they act as trustees and review his proposals. This definition also prevails with regard to community intervention. Citizens do not expect to be continuously involved. They react to policy proposals or changes. Wellesley's budgetary process and the influence of representatives was distinctive because the committee and superintendent did not concur. They had to find a way, through the community, of resolving their conflicts. Yet all the committees did precipitate some reaction to the superintendents' proposals. Their responses were defensive, although recognizing that the reactions were not representative of the whole community. They felt it necessary to stay further public confrontations. Therefore they accepted retaining the implementation of programs such as the state lunch, even in times of financial stringency.

Taking financial decisions does differ greatly from that of educational policy decisions. It had seemed possible that it could differ because financial decisions do not ostensibly require knowledge of education. However, they are not seen as simpler or more susceptible to citizen control and are also regarded as requiring an expertise. The municipal or school representatives only set the parameters by specifying ceilings or guidelines; they do not deal with the detail. Specifically, they refrain from pronouncements upon the instructional programs. Their areas of intervention are strictly non-educational. Even here, there are limits to the involvement. Input is sporadic, generally a reaction to the superintendent's proposals rather than an initiative.

The definition of professional control is not as simple as had been presumed. It does not merely relate to educational matters but also to administrative and technical issues. It is further complicated because in one area of decision-making—that of salaries—there is a difference of approach. Even here a form of professional control does prevail. In salary negotiations it is the teacher associations rather than the superintendents that appear to exert considerable influence over the decision-making process and its outcome. The local nature and division of labor in American education really mean that a very narrow set of participants have the means to control the daily workings of the system. Their powers are not unbounded, and, by inspection of the process of collective bargaining, evidence does emerge that their areas of discretion are slowly being eroded. In respect to salary negotiations, the superintendent is no longer in the same supreme position as he was before the advent of collective bargaining. Then he had virtual autocratic control over the interest groups producing the educational process—teachers and administrators—as well as the ability to influence the decision-making process of the school committees. Collective bargaining has led to larger organizations of teachers, often on a regional basis. By these collective strategies they are able to counteract the influence that other professional educators—the superintendents—wield over them. There have been a number of stark instances of this occurring in the large cities.[8] This study confirms the prevalence of the mood of change in the suburbs.

Professional control of local education in America is very special. It is evident that it does not just refer to instructional matters such as decisions on curriculum content and developments. It is more extensive, relating to the many decisions about the directions and management of the system that are not purely educational in content. It is not concerned only with esoteric matters of the educational system.[9] It extends to matters such as defining the ways in which the community may participate in the decision-making process. It is also concerned with non-educational matters because of the general social division of labor. The elected representatives and lay citizens cannot get intimately involved in the decision-making process not only because of situational factors, such as lack of requisite expertise or the available time, but also because of their beliefs in the way the system should run. The result is that the representatives pursue ad hoc and rather random methods of inspection over the professional educators, methods which leave the administrators free to direct the system. The strategies for professional control in American education now involve managerial as well as educational practices.

Indeed with the development of collective bargaining the managerial practices are becoming more predominant in the educational process. The superintendents no longer have a body of professional educators over whom they are the charismatic and educational leaders. The superintendents are now not accepted merely by dint of their educational skills or expertise. The teachers no longer see that the superintendents have the same set of interests as themselves and are less willing to accept the superintendent as their spokesman on educational matters. The superintendent is seen as an agent of management rather than a member of the teaching body. The superintendents' educational tasks are more difficult to pursue. Also it is no longer vital that the superintendent display educational expertise in order to be appointed to such a position. Rather, the requisite skills are managerial and political. The subordinate administrators—particularly the associate superintendents—display, in these four communities, more knowledge of the educational process and the academic skills that are necessary than the superintendents.[10] The superintendents have been developing techniques such as program budgeting and have tried to adopt more positivistic methods of evaluation of their school systems. Training programs for school administrators accentuate these skills.[11] But there is not yet evidence of the improved success of school systems as a result.

What emerges from this study is that an organization of the educational system providing formal opportunities for citizen participation by means of community size or government machinery does not produce much more citizen involvement than a more traditional bureaucratic structure. It may, however, help prevent frustrations with the system. Professional control in education may be pervasive not because of the topics but because of general organization of work and political activities in a modern industrial society. Citizens in communities do not take an active part in the decision-making process for many reasons, none of which are adequately specified by this study of decision processes. It would require an intensive survey of citizen attitudes to arrive at definitive explanations.

There are, however, two possible sets of explanations. One has to do with the structure of the situation and the other, the attitudes held to uphold the present organization. Structural variables that may prevent participation are the organization of work into full-time occupations, whereby citizens have little free time. Secondly, the school system may be organized so that the key decisions are not taken either locally or regularly, thus preventing the effectiveness of a participatory strategy. Indeed, there is much evidence that pressure is exerted much more inconspicuously either by a local elite or elites or more centrally through the operations of the economy and its needs for labor.[12] Studies of educational effects increasingly demonstrate that the most important purposes are to provide for the necessary skills in the economy or to socialize children to society's moral values.

The attitudinal variables preventing participation are threefold. Citizens may not perceive a need to intervene at a particular point in time, although they accept the legitimacy of participation. They may well be satisfied with the character of the system. Second, they may not feel that they could effectively intervene. The machinery or the type of decision may preclude effective participation. Hamilton, for example, argues that public knowledge of political issues is great and that there is a latent demand for radical change that has not been tapped by political organization.[13] Third and perhaps most important, citizens may not accept the legitimacy of participation. They may well accept the notion of a representative rather than participatory democracy whereby their attitudes are fed into the system through the electoral process.[14]

The implications of changing the structure of the educational system to allow for more citizen participation are clear. A mere change in size or governmental machinery would not have much effect on the relations between citizens and professional educators. However, the size variable studied may, in fact, not be sufficiently discriminating since the smallest population was of 10,000 citizens. It may be necessary to have a very small community of a few hundred families to ensure that the citizens do more than merely ratify the decisions and set the boundaries within which the professional educators work. Mansbridge's study, however, did not point up the success of a town meeting form of democracy in a very small rural area.[15]

My study points to the pervasiveness of professionalism and confirms the findings of studies of the large cities in the USA which indicate that the political culture of the area, although affecting decision processes by making for more or less community interaction, does not seriously affect outcomes.[16] The decentralization of the New York City school district, for example, has been shown not to be very successful, although the majority of the citizens of the constituent neighborhoods were in favor of such a move:

> The enormous emphasis on professionalism has greatly undermined the role of the lay citizenry in the policy process. A major element in the alienation of large segments of the city population is the great reliance on professionalism that is integral to the reform ethos.[17]

Indeed, there can be little hope that more radical alternatives proposed, such as education vouchers to provide more parental choice, will have any greater effect on changing the locus of control.[18] In the present complex societies, it cannot be expected that citizens would do more than adjudicate on the efficacy and efficiency of a school system. The problem is that the educational system is not the key organizational feature of modern industrial society. It is merely the mechanism by which individuals are socialized into the social system. The sources of control are elsewhere and determine, rather than are determined by, the structure of the educational system. Changes in administrative arrangements may not yield critical developments to relations between lay citizens and professionals.

NOTES TO CHAPTER NINE

1. The key studies which pointed up professional control over types of policy were Norman Kerr, "The School Board as an Agent of Legitimation," *Sociology of Education*, (Fall 1964), pp. 34–59; Roscoe Martin,

Government and the Suburban School (Syracuse: Syracuse University Press, 1962); David Minar, *Decision Making in Suburban Communities* (Evanston: Northwestern University, 1966).

2. Edward Banfield, *Political Influence* (New York: Free Press, 1963), p. 7; P. Bachrach and M. Baratz, *Power and Poverty* (New York:OUP, 1970), p. 9.

3. Statement from interview with Mr. Charles Sweeny of Quincy, in Boston, January 19, 1973.

4. For different notions and explanations of representation see Hannah Pitkin, *The Concept of Representation* (Berkeley: University of California Press, 1967).

5. For a more detailed discussion of the trend in attitudes, see George E. Peterson and Arthur P. Solomon, "Property Taxes and Populist Reform," *Public Interest* (Winter 1973), pp. 60–75.

6. Donald McCarty and J.E. Ramsey *The School Managers* (Westport, Ct.: Greenwood, 1971), p. 20 passim.

7. Norman Kerr, *op. cit.,* coined the term for this general activity.

8. See, particularly, Maurice Berube and Marilyn Gittell (eds.), *Confrontation at Oceanhill-Brownsville.* (New York: Praeger, 1968) and Melvin Urovfsky (ed.), *Why Teachers Strike* (New York: Doubleday, Anchor, 1970).

9. Roscoe Martin, *op. cit.,* elaborated this distinction between esoteric and exoteric issues in educational decisions.

10. Interviews with Drs. Phinney, Bachelder, Muto and Stayn, December 1972 and January 1973.

11. Many of the training programs teach courses in management and PPBS. Some—for example, the Administrative Career Program at Harvard Graduate School of Education—have joint arrangements with neighboring Business Schools.

12. The political science debate centered on theories of elite versus pluralist local power structures. See particularly Ramsey and McCarty's summary, *op. cit.,* introduction. More recently research has been conducted on the effects of schooling. See especially C. Jencks, et al., *Inequality: A Reassessment of the Effects of Family and Schooling in America* (New York: Basic Books, 1972).

13. H.S. Hamilton, *Class & Politics in the USA* (New York: Wiley 1972) especially p. 15.

14. See, for example, J.E. Horton and W.E. Thompson, "Powerlessness and Political Negativism: A Study of Defeated Local Referendums," *American Journal of Sociology* (March 1962), pp. 485–493; L.H. Massotti, *Patterns of White and Non White School Referenda Participation and Support: Cleveland 1960-1964,* In M. Gittell (ed.), *Educating an Urban Population* (Beverly Hills: Sage, 1967), pp. 240–256; H. Summerfield, *The Neighborhood-based Politics of Education* (Columbus, Ohio: Merrill, 1971); N. Gross, et al., *Who Runs our Schools?* (New York: Wiley, 1958).

15. Jane Mansbridge, *Town Meeting Democracy*. Working Papers for a New
    Society, Vol. 1, No. 2, Summer 1973.
16. M. Gittell and T.E. Hollander, *Six Demonstration School Districts*. (New
    York: Praeger, 1969) and H. Thomas James, "The School Budgetary
    Process of Large Cities." In A. Rosenthal (ed.), *Governing Education*
    (Garden City: Doubleday, 1969).
17. Gittell and Berube, *op. cit.,* p. 331.
18. G.R. La Noue (ed.), *Education Vouchers: Concepts and Controversies*
    (New York: Teachers College Press, 1972).

Bibliography

Alford, R.A. *Bureaucracy and Participation.* Chicago: Rand McNally, 1969.

Almond, G. and S. Verba. *The Civic Culture.* Boston: Little Brown, 1969.

Altshuler, A. *Community Control.* New York: Pegasus, 1970.

Argyris, C. *Intervention Theory and Method.* Reading, Mass.: Addison-Wesley, 1970.

Bachrach, P. and M. Baratz. *Power and Poverty: Theory and Practice,* London: Oxford University Press, 1970.

Bailey, S. and E. Mosher. *ESEA - The Office of Education Administers a Law.* Syracuse, N.Y.: Syracuse University Press, 1967.

Bailyn, B. *Education in the Forming of American Society.* Chapel Hill: University of North Carolina Press, 1960.

Banfield, E. (ed.) *Political Influence.* New York: Free Press, 1961. *Urban Government.* New York: Free Press, 1969.

Banks, O. *Sociology of Education.* London: Batsford, 1967.

Barber, J.D. *Power in Committees.* Chicago: Rand McNally, 1966.

Bendiner, R. *The Politics of Schools.* New York: Harper & Row, 1969.

Berube, M. and M. Gittell. *Confrontation at Ocean Hill-Brownsville.* New York: Praeger, 1968.

Bloomberg, W. and M. Sunshine. *Suburban Power Structures—Public Education: A Study of Values, Influence and Tax Effort.* Syracuse: Syracuse University Press, 1963.

Bowers, C.A., I. Housego and Doris Dyke. (eds.) *Education and Social Policy.* New York: Random House, 1970.

Braybrooke, D. and C.E. Lindblom. *A Strategy of Decision.* New York: Free Press, 1963.

Burkhead, Jesse. *State and Local Taxes for Public Education.* Syracuse: Syracuse University Press, 1963.

Cahill, R.S. and S.P. Hencley. (eds.) *The Politics of Education in the Local Community.* Danville: Interstate, 1964.

Callahan, R.E. *Education and the Cult of Efficiency.* Chicago: University of Chicago Press, 1962.

Campbell, Roald, et al. *The Organization and Control of American Schools.* Columbus, Ohio: Merrill, 1967.

Carlson, R.O. *Executive Succession.* Columbus, Ohio: Merrill, 1972.

Cohen, David. "The Price of Community Control" *Commentary, 1969,* pp. 23-32.

Coleman, J. *Community Conflict.* Glencoe: Free Press, 1957.

Coons, John E., W.H. Clune, and S.D. Sugarman. *Private Wealth and Public Education.* Cambridge, Mass.: Belknap, 1970.

Corwin, R.E. *A Sociology of Education.* New York: Appleton Century Crofts, 1965.

Crain, Robert L. *The Politics of School Desegregation.* Chicago: Aldine, 1968.

Crecine, John P. (ed.) *Financing the Metropolis.* Chicago: Aldine, 1968.

Cremin, L. *The Transformation of the School.* New York: Knopf, 1961.

Cronin, J. *The Control of American Schools.* Boston: Little Brown, 1973.

Dahl, R.A. *Preface to Democratic Theory.* Chicago: University of Chicago Press, 1956. *Who Governs?* New Haven: Yale University Press, 1957.

Deutsch, Karl. *Nerves of Government.* New York: Free Press, 1963.

Eliot, T.H. "Towards an Understanding of Public School Politics", *American Political Science Review,* 1959, p. 50.

Etzioni, A. *The Semi Professions and Their Organization: Teachers, Nurses and Social Workers.* New York: Free Press, 1969.

Finn, C. and L. Lenkowsky. " 'Serrano' Versus the People", *Commentary,* September 1972, Vol. 52, pp. 68-72.

Fein, L.J. *The Ecology of the Public Schools.* New York: Pegasus, 1971.

Franke, D. & H. *Safe Places of the U.S.A.* New York: Arlington House, 1972.

Friedrich, C. *Man and his Government.* New York: McGraw Hill, 1963.

Gans, H. *The Levittowners.* New York: Pantheon, 1967.

Geel, Tyl van. *Efficiency, Effectiveness and Local School Systems.* Unpublished doctoral dissertation, Harvard Graduate School of Education, 1972.

Gittell, M. *Participants and Participation.* New York: Center for Urban Education, 1966. *Educating an Urban Population.* Beverley Hills: Sage, 1967.

Gittell, M. and A.G. Hevesi (eds.) *The Politics of Urban Education.* New York: Praeger, 1969.

Gittell, M. and T.E. Hollander. 6 *Demonstration School Districts.* New York: Praeger, 1968.

Goss, E. *The History of Melrose.* Massachusetts: City of Melrose, 1902.

Glazer, N. and D.P. Moynihan. *Beyond the Melting Pot.* Cambridge, Mass.: MIT Press, 1963.

Goldhammer, K. *The School Board.* New York: Center for Applied Research in Education, 1966.

Goode, William J. "Encroachment, Charlatanism and the Emerging Profession," *American Sociological Review,* 1960, Vol. 25, pp. 902-913.

Griffiths, D.E. *Administrative Theory.* New York: Appleton-Century-Crofts,

1959. *The School Superintendent.* New York: Center for Applied Education, 1966.

Gross, N. *Explorations in Role Analysis.* New York: Wiley, 1958. *Who Runs our Schools?* New York: Wiley, 1958.

Halpin, A.W. (ed.) *Administrative Theory in Education.* Chicago: Midwest Administration Center, University of Chicago, 1958.

Hamilton, R.F. *Class & Politics in the USA.* New York: Wiley, 1972.

Havinghurst, Robert. *Education in Metropolitan Areas.* Boston: Allyn and Bacon, 1966.

Hays, Sam. *Municipal Reform in the Progressive Era: In Whose Class Interest?* Boston: New England Free Press, 1972.

Hunter, Floyd. *The Community Power Structure.* Chapel Hill: University of North Carolina Press, 1953.

Iannaccone, L. *Politics in Education.* New York: Center for Applied Research in Education, 1967.

Iannaccone, L. and F.W. Lutz. *Power, Politics and Policy: The Governing of Local School Districts.* Columbus, Ohio: Merrill, 1970.

James, H.T. "Politics and Community Decision-Making in Education." *Review of Educational Research,* October 1967, Vol. 31, pp. 377–386.

James, H.T., James A. Kelly and Walter Garms. *Determinants of Educational Expenditures in Large Cities of the U.S.* US Dept. of Health, Education and Welfare. Office of Education Cooperative Research Project No. 2389 (Stanford, Calif.: School of Education, Stanford University, 1966.)

Jencks, C. et al. *Inequality.* New York: Basic Books, 1972.

Johnson, Terence. *Professions and Power.* London: MacMillan, 1972.

Katz, M. (ed.) *Class, Bureaucracy and the Schools.* New York: Praeger, 1971. *School Reform: Past and Present.* Boston: Little Brown, 1971.

Kerr, N. "The School Board as an Agent of Legitimation," *Sociology of Education,* Fall 1964, Vol. 38, pp. 34–59.

Kimborough, Ralph. *Political Power and Educational Decision Making.* Chicago: Rand McNally, 1964.

Kirst, M. (ed.) *The Politics of Education at the Local, State, and Federal Levels.* Berkeley: McCutchan, 1970.

Kirst, M. (ed.) *State, School and Politics.* Lexington, Mass. D.C. Heath, 1972.

Kirst, M. and F. Wirt. *The Political Web of American Schools.* Boston: Little Brown, 1972.

Koerner, J. *Who Controls American Education?* Boston: Beacon, 1968.

LaNoue, G.R. (ed.) *Education Vouchers: Concepts and Controversies.* New York: Teachers College Press, 1972.

Lazerson, Marvin and D. Cohen. "Education and the Corporate Order" *Socialist Revolution,* March–April 1972, Vol. 2, pp. 47–72.

Lekachman, R. "Schools, Money and Politics: Financing Public Education." *The New Leader,* September 1972, pp. 69–89.

Levin, H. (ed.) *Community Control of Schools.* New York: Simon and Schuster, 1970.

Lindblom, C. "The Science of Muddling Through." *Public Administration, Review,* 1952, Vol. 12, pp. 79–88.

Lipset, S.M. *Political Man.* Garden City: Doubleday, 1959. *Ideology of Local Control.* In C.A. Bowers, I. Housego, and Doris Dyke (eds.), *Education and Social Policy.* New York: Random House, 1970.

Lipsky, M. *Protest in City Politics: Rent Strikes, Housing and the Power of the Poor.* Chicago: Rand McNally, 1970.

Locke, M. *The Politics of Education.* London: Routledge, Kegan Paul 1973.

Lutz, F. and J. Assarelli. (eds.) *The Struggle for Power in Education.* Washington, D.C.: Center for Applied Research in Education, 1966.

Mansbridge, J.J. "Town Meeting Democracy", *Working Papers for a New Society,* 1973, Vol. 1, No. 2, pp. 5–15.

Marshall, T.H. *Sociology at the Crossroads.* London: Heineman, 1963.

Martin, R.C. *Government and the Suburban School.* Syracuse, N.Y.: Syracuse University Press, 1962.

Marris, Peter and M. Rein. *Dilemmas of Social Reform.* London: Routledge and Kegan Paul, 1973. (2nd ed.)

Masters, N. et al. *State Politics and Public Schools.* New York: Knopf, 1964.

Masotti, Louis H. *Education and Politics in Suburbia.* Cleveland: The Press of Western Reserve University, 1967.

McCarty, D. and J.E. Ramsey. *The School Managers.* Westport, Ct.: Greenwood, 1971.

Miller, D. "Governing Child Care Centers." In P. Roby (ed.), *Child Care: Who Cares?* New York: Basic Books, 1973.

Miller, S.M. and P. Roby. *The Future of Inequality.* New York: Basic Books, 1970.

Mills, C.W. *The Power Elite.* New York: Oxford University Press, 1956.

Minar, D. *Decision Making in Suburban Communities.* Evanston, Ill.: Northwestern University Press 1966.

Miner, J. *Social and Economic Factors in Spending on Public Education.* Syracuse: Syracuse University Press, 1963.

Moynihan, Daniel P. (ed.) *On Understanding Poverty.* New York: Basic Books, 1968. *Maximum Feasible Misunderstanding.* New York: Free Press, 1971. "Equalizing Education: In Whose Benefit?" *The Public Interest,* Fall 1972, Vol. 29, pp. 69–90.

Murphy, Jerome. "Title 1: Bureaucratic Politics and Poverty Politics." *Inequality in Education,* 1973, Vol. 6, pp. 9–15.

Myers, C. *Collective Bargaining for Teachers.* Lexington, Mass.: D.C. Heath, 1972.

Perry, C.R. and W.A. Wildman. *The Impact of Negotiations on Public Education.* Worthington, Ohio: James, 1970.

Peterson, Paul. "Forms of Representation: Participation of the Poor in the Community Action Program," *American Political Science Review,* 1970, Vol. 64, No. 2, pp. 491–507.

Peterson, Paul and Paul Kantor. *Partisanship and the Limits of Democratic Theory.* Unpublished paper, University of Chicago, 1970.

Peterson, G. and A. Soloman, "Property Taxes and Populist Reform," *Public Interest,* Winter 1973, Vol. 30, pp. 60–75.

Pitkin, Hannah. *The Concept of Representation.* Berkeley: University of California Press, 1967.

Piven, Francis Fox and R. Cloward. *Regulating the Poor.* New York: Random House, 1971.

Pois, Joseph. *The School Board Crisis.* Chicago: Educational Methods Inc., 1964.

Polsby, Norman. *Community Power and Political Theory.* New Haven: Yale University Press, 1963.

Rivlin, Alice. *Systematic Thinking for Social Action,* Washington, D.C.: Brookings Institution, 1971.

Reller, T.L. *The Development of the City Superintendency of Schools.* Philadelphia: Author, 1935.

Rogers, David. *110, Livingston Street.* New York: Vintage Books, 1969.

Rosenthal, Alan. "Teacher Administrator Relations: Harmony or Conflict?" *Public Administration Review,* June 1967, pp. 154–161. (ed.) *Governing Education.* New York: Doubleday, 1968. *Pedagogues and Power.* Syracuse: Syracuse University Press, 1969.

Sayre, Wallace and H. Kaufman. *Governing New York City.* New York: Norton, 1965.

Schultze, C. *The Politics and Economy of Public Spending.* Washington, D.C.: Brooking's Institution, 1968.

Schrag, Peter. *Village School Downtown.* Boston: Beacon, 1967.

Schultze, C. et al. *Setting National Priorities: The 1973 Budget.* Washington, D.C.: Brooking's Institution, 1972.

Simon, H.A. *Administrative Behavior.* New York: MacMillan, 1959.

Sharkansky, Ira. *Spending in the American States.* Chicago: Rand McNally, 1969.

Summerfield, Harry. *The Neighborhood Based Politics of Education.* Columbus, Ohio: Merrill, 1971.

Urofsky, M. (ed.) *Why Teachers Strike.* New York: Anchor, Doubleday, 1970.

Vidich, A. and J. Bensman. *Small Town in Mass Society.* Princeton: Princeton University Press, 1958.

Walton, J. *Administration and Policy Making in Education.* Baltimore: Johns Hopkins Press, 1959.

Weber, Max. *Theory of Economic and Social Organization.* New York: Free Press of Glencoe, 1956.

Whitehead, Clay. *Uses and Limitations of Systems Analysis.* Santa Monica, Ca.: Rand Corporation, 1967.

Wildavsky, Aaron. *The Politics of the Budgetary Process.* Boston: Little Brown, 1964.

Wildavsky, Aaron and A.J. Meltsner, "Leave City Budgeting Alone!" In J. Crecine, *Financing the Metropolis,* Chicago: Aldine, 1968.

Wilensky, Harold. "The Professionalization of Everyone?" *American Journal of Sociology,* 1964, Vol. 69, pp. 137–158.

Wood, Robert C. *Suburbia: Its People and Their Politics.* Boston: Houghton Mifflin, 1958.

Index

arbitration, 108

Banfield, E., 127
Barber, J.D., 5, 35; allocation of revenue, 13
Britain: teachers, 4
budgets: in Barber, 5, 35; definition of
  operating, 41; defined by Wildavsky, 11;
  eighteen-month, 46, 52; effects of tax
  base, 21; nature of cuts, 122; review
  strategy, 60, 68; role of city/town
  government, 118, 119; salary negotiations, 23
building program, 45

collective bargaining, 102, 135; and budgeting, 14; Melrose, 34; and power, 139; in
  Quincy, 62
community participation, 80, 135; concept
  of, 15; influence delineation, 128;
  priorities, 86; salary negotiations, 106;
  107, size and political mode, 140
control, professional, 4; concept of, 139

decisionmaking: and collective bargaining,
  108, 109; concept of in education, 131;
  influence, 22; political characteristics,
  125; professional educators, 6; in school
  committee, 137

education: conflicting roles, 110; labor
  intensive, 113; role of, 2
ESEA (Elementary and Secondary Education Act), 2; Melrose, 33

fiscal autonomy: concept of, 18; local
  school committee, 134; school committees, 42; town/municipal control, 118

funding: court cases, 3

Goode, W.J., 4
Goss, E.H., 28
Gross, N., 19, 72
group pressure, 92

Hamilton, A.S., 17, 140
Hell, M.G., 16

innovations, 52
instructional program, 52
interaction: and political culture, 141;
  theory of, 137
IPT (Instructional Planning Team), 48;
  bargaining, 110

James, H.T., 25; public officials and budget
  process, 47; revenue, 21

Kerr, N., 7
Kirst, M., 5, 18; and Wirt, F., 110

Lipset, S.M., 85, 86
LMT (Learning Management Team), 49

McCarthy, D. and Ramsey, J.E., 6, 139
Mansbridge, J., 141
Martin, R., 7, 17
Massachusetts: budget cycle, 16; fiscal
  autonomy, 18
MEA (Melrose Education Association),
  33, 104
Melrose: alderman and budget, 120; budget
  procedure, 48; budget review, 65; community interaction, 74; description, 20;
  open budget meeting, 81, 82; pressure

About the Author

Miriam E. David is lecturer in Social Administration at the University of Bristol. She has conducted social research at London University in psychiatry, gambling, and educational policy.

After teaching courses in sociology and statistics at London University, Ms. David was appointed visiting research associate at the Harvard Graduate School of Education, where this book was undertaken.

She is currently engaged in writing on the educational system in Great Britain.